Get Veterinary School

MW01029801

Insights by an Admissions Expert

Third Edition

For High School, College & Returning Adult Students

Joseph M. Piekunka, M.S. Ed.

Acknowledgements

The author would like to acknowledge both the American Veterinary Medical Association (AVMA) and the Association of American Veterinary Medical Colleges (AAVMC) for allowing him to reprint portions of their material, some of which is copyrighted. This material has helped this book be both more informative and more useful to pre-veterinary students, their parents, and their advisors.

The author would also like to acknowledge his editor, Dr. Burke Hilsabeck, who not only edited this book; he made useful suggestions on how to enhance the messages within.

Copyright © 2015 by Joseph M. Piekunka
Published by Lulu Press, Inc.
All rights reserved.
USBN: 978-1-329-25495-4

This book is dedicated to...

The memory of Priscilla Schenck, who was my administrative assistant for ten years at Cornell University, a valued colleague, and my friend. She was liked by faculty, staff, and students alike at Cornell. It has been difficult to accept a world without Priscilla. She is truly missed by all who knew her well.

Acronyms Used in Veterinary Schools and This Book

AAVMC®	Association of American Veterinary Medical Colleges
AJVR®	American Journal of Veterinary Research
AVMA®	American Veterinary Medical Association
APVMA	American Pre-Veterinary Medical Association
BA/BS	Bachelor of Arts/Bachelor of Science
CLEP®	College Level Examination Program
CDC	Centers for Disease Control, U.S. Dept. of HHS
CVM	College of Veterinary Medicine
CVMA	Canadian Veterinary Medical Association
DVM	Doctor of Veterinary Medicine
ELoR	Electronic Letter of Recommendation (by VMCAS)
ETS®	Educational Testing Service
FAO	Financial Aid Office
FVM	Faculty of Veterinary Medicine
FVS	Faculty of Veterinary Science or Studies
GRE®	Graduate Record Exam, General Test, from ETS
JAVMA®	Journal of AVMA
JVME®	Journal of Veterinary Medical Education
MA/MS	Master of Arts/Master of Science
MCAT®	Medical College Admissions Test
MD	Medical Doctor, Physician of Allopathic Medicine
NAAHP	National Assoc. of Advisors for the Health Professions
	CAAHP Central Association of Advisors…
	NEAAHP Northeastern Association of Advisors…
	SAAHP Southern Association of Advisors…
	WAAHP Western Association of Advisors…
NIH	National Institutes of Health, U.S. Dept. of HHS
PPI	Personal Potential Index, by ETS
SAT	Scholastic Aptitude Test (PSAT—Preliminary SAT)
SCAVMA	Student Chapter of the AVMA (at each CVM & SVM)
SVM	School of Veterinary Medicine
TOEFL®	Test of English as a Foreign Language
VHS	Veterinary Health Sciences
VMCAS	Veterinary Medical College Application Service
VMD	Veterinary Medical Doctor
VMSAR	Veterinary Medical School Admission Requirements
VCAT®	Veterinary College Admissions Test, discontinued
VSTP	Veterinary Scientist Training Program—DVM/PhD
WICHE	Western Interstate Consortium of Higher Education

Contents

Chapters

Appendices:

Table 1A: Veterinary Colleges of the American Association of Veterinary Medical Colleges (AAVMC)

U.S. University or College	College Name or Abbreviation
Auburn University (Alabama)	CVM (College of Veterinary Med.)
Colorado State University	CVM and Biomedical Sciences
Cornell University (NY)	CVM
Iowa State University	CVM
Kansas State University	CVM
Lincoln Memorial Univ. (TN)	CVM
Louisiana State University	SVM (School of Veterinary Med.)
Michigan State University	CVM
Midwestern University (AZ)	CVM
Mississippi State University	CVM
North Carolina State University	CVM
The Ohio State University	CVM
Oklahoma State University	CVM & Veterinary Health Science Ctr
Oregon State University	CVM
Purdue University (Indiana)	SVM
Texas A & M University	CVM
Tufts University (MA)	Cummings SVM
Tuskegee University (Alabama)	SVM
University of California-Davis	SVM
University of Florida	CVM
University of Georgia	CVM
University of Illinois-Urbana	CVM
University of Minnesota	CVM
University of Missouri	Columbia CVM
University of Pennsylvania	SVM
University of Tennessee	CVM
University of Wisconsin-Madison	SVM
Virginia-Maryland Regional Coll.	CVM (at Virginia Polytechnic.)
Washington State University	CVM
Western Univ. of Health Sciences	CVM (California)

Canada	
University of Calgary (Alberta)	FVM (Faculty of Veterinary Med.)
University of Guelph (Ontario)	Ontario VC
Université de Montreal (Québec)	FVM
University of Prince Edward Is.	Atlantic VC
University of Saskatchewan	Western CVM

Table 1B: International Veterinary Colleges of the AAVMC

Region & Country/Isle	University Name	College Name or Abbreviation
Central America		
Cayman Is.	Saint Matthew's Univ.	SVM
Costa Rica	Universidad VERITAS	SVM
Grenada	Saint George's Univ.	SVM
Mexico	National Autonomous Univ. of Mexico (UNAM)	CVM/FMV
Saint Kitts	Ross University	SVM
Europe		
Denmark	Univ. of Copenhagen	Faculty of Life Sciences
Ireland	University Coll. Dublin	VM Degree Programme
Netherlands	Utrecht University	FVM
UK England	University of London	Royal VC
UK Scotland	Univ. of Edinburgh	Royal SV Studies
UK Scotland	University of Glasgow	SVM
Pacific		
Australia	Melbourne University	FVS
Australia	Murdoch University	SV & Biomed. Sciences
Australia	University of Queensland	SV Science
Australia	University of Sydney	FVS
Japan	University of Tokyo	Agricultural & Life Sciences
New Zealand	Massey University	VS (IVABS)
Philippines	Central Luzon State Univ.	CVSM
South Korea	Seoul National University	FVS

Abbreviations

Like all professions, there are many acronyms used in veterinary medicine. "CVM" is widely used in the U.S. to mean both a college and a school of veterinary medicine, even though there is a separate abbreviation, (SVM) for school. "DVM" is also used widely to mean veterinarian. The University of Pennsylvania confers degrees in Latin, and thus uses the abbreviation VMD. When we use DVM, we also imply VMD. We broadly use "CVM" to include all colleges, schools, and faculties of veterinary medicine. Likewise, we broadly use the "DVM" to include all veterinarians, regardless of degrees issued in Latin or English. Thank you for understanding our need for brevity.

Foreword

There is a significant amount of academic and other work that is required to become a veterinarian. Much of this work will be required of you before you even apply to veterinary school. This book is intended to help you get started and to help you plan a comprehensive approach to preparing for veterinary school.

This book is not intended to discourage students. Yet some of the realities of preparing for veterinary school may be unrealized by some students. The book will take a no-non-sense approach to advising you. If you find the information in this book discouraging, please do not give up. Read this book and then talk with a local veterinarian or two. Ask what their veterinary preparation experience was like.

There is a lot of factual information available to aspiring veterinarians. The Association of American Veterinary Medical Colleges (AAVMC) gathers and distributes admissions facts and details. They post most, if not all, of their information at aavmc.org and in the book *Veterinary Medical School Admission Requirements* (VMSAR). You can access these resources of the AAVMC at aavmc.org as well as those of the American Veterinary Medical Association at avma.org. You can also browse online book stores for books on careers with animals. Remember, not everyone who works with animals is a veterinarian.

The sad truth about veterinary medicine admissions is that more applicants will be denied admission than will be enrolled at each college. Students have been denied admission simply because there are not enough seats for all of the talented students who wish to pursue the profession. This fact was one motivation for writing a book that contains advice and guidance and not just admissions facts.

About the Author

The author has over three decades of experience in higher education admissions beginning in 1982. He has served in a number of admissions capacities, including:

1986–1990	Director of Graduate Admissions
	Queens College, City University of New York
1990–1995	Assistant Vice Provost for Graduate Admissions & Records
	Binghamton University, State University of New York
1995–2005	Director of DVM Admissions
	College of Veterinary Medicine, Cornell University
2005–	President & Founder, PreVetAdvising.com
2011–2012	Ind. Contractor, created the *Pre-Vet Advisor Newsletter*
	Association of American Veterinary Medical Colleges

He is or has been a member of many professional organizations including:
The National Association of Advisors for the Health Professions
The Northeastern Association of Advisors for the Health Professions
The National Association of Graduate Admissions Professionals
The State University of New York College of Admissions Professionals
The American Association of Collegiate Registrars & Admissions Officers
The Council of Graduate Schools
The National Association of College Admissions Counselors

About the Data in This Book

The school-specific data tables in this book are meant to supplement the advice given. These data are not necessarily the most current data or the most comprehensive. In some cases, we have intentionally printed out-of-date data, particularly when listing deadlines. This is done solely to provide current applicants with an incentive to find the most recent information in the *Veterinary Medical School Admission Requirements* (VMSAR) or at aavmc.org.

We strongly suggest that every reader find or buy a copy of the VMSAR as he or she approaches to the time of application to veterinary school. It is a very useful book. Most pre-health advisors will have a current copy. VMSAR is published annually and the most recent edition is usually available in May in your campus bookstore or online. Please view the data tables in this book as a supplement to our advice and not as the most current information for students applying to veterinary school in the near term.

Introduction

It is hoped that this book will help the reader understand how to become a competitive applicant to veterinary schools across North America. There are many students preparing for the veterinary profession who do not have a pre-veterinary advisor. There are two large groups of students without adequate pre-veterinary advising. The first group is high school students. Guidance counselors (also referred to as college counselors) are often not up-to-date about the smaller professions, particularly those professions that require graduate-level education. These counselors are busy with heavy caseloads and with understanding the undergraduate admissions world; it is very difficult for them to learn how to advise pre-veterinary students. This book is intended to help guidance counselors, high school pre-veterinary students, college-level pre-veterinary students, and their advisors and parents.

Another large audience for this book is returning adult students, often referred to as the non-traditional students, who may be changing careers or who have always wanted to be veterinarians but were detoured during or after college by unanticipated events or circumstances. Returning adult students often feel disconnected from the academic world, which is where good pre-veterinary advising is available. Many adult students take classes at night or on weekends when advising offices are typically closed. This book is also meant to help returning adult students in understanding the many hoops that one must jump through to get into veterinary school.

A third and usually better informed audience is college-level pre-veterinary students. Most of these students have access to a pre-health advisor, or at large universities, to a pre-veterinary advisor. This book may also be helpful to traditional college students. There are many small liberal arts colleges where pre-health advising is distributed among the faculty and no central pre-health advising is available. The faculty members on these smaller campuses are often well-informed about the larger health professions, but some may not be adequately informed to advise students who are preparing for a smaller health profession, like veterinary medicine.

It is hoped that our book and the corresponding consulting service will help to fill a void. In the world of human medicine, there are dozens of books of advice and admissions consulting firms that help pre-medical students gain admission to medical school. The same is not true of veterinary medicine. At the time of the writing of this edition, nothing has been written for North American pre-veterinary students except this book. *Veterinary Medical School Admission Requirements* (VMSAR) does not provide students with advice; it lists admissions facts and figures.

Our book should give you comprehensive advice in all realms of admissions preparation, including academic preparation, animal and veterinary experience, extracurricular experience, and specific help for interviews, essays and applications. The author, the father of a high school student and college student, gives very practical advice for all age groups preparing for veterinary medicine.

Do you love animals, people, and science equally?

Everyone acknowledges that any student who is thinking about a career in veterinary medicine should love animals. Some students are attracted to the profession because they want to work with animals more than people. Nevertheless, most animals are attached to a client who pays the veterinarian's bills. There are also people who work in veterinary clinics and hospitals with whom veterinarians need to work. As a veterinarian, you will have to give bad news to your clients from time to time. You need to like and have compassion for people. If you are choosing veterinary medicine in order to avoid people, think again. You should love working with people just as much as you love working with animals.

Likewise, a love of science would help you to be a better veterinarian. Science—and math—are essential to the veterinary profession, and you should have an appreciation for these subjects as a pre-veterinary student. As a veterinarian, you will frequently encounter diseases and cases that require you to analyze and process information as a scientist. If you dislike science, veterinary medicine probably is not the right choice for you.

A love of animals alone will not heal the animals that you see. However, a love of animals, people, and science together will make you the best veterinarian that you can be.

One additional consideration is your ability to deal with the deaths of animals. As a veterinarian, you will encounter clients who do not have enough money to pay for the basic procedures that must be done to save their pets. You will know that you can save the animal if you are given the opportunity, yet you may be asked to put the animal to sleep. This author personally knows a small number of veterinarians who spent over one hundred thousand dollars on their undergraduate and DVM degrees and then realized, after less than a dozen years in the profession, that this was a reality and left the profession. Death is difficult to deal with, especially when it is medically avoidable.

For many students, death, especially as a financial alternative to relatively inexpensive medical procedures, is difficult to accept. If you cannot see yourself putting to sleep animals that you know you could save, you may wish to reconsider your professional path. In the great majority of cases, the veterinarian is a healer, but sometimes the veterinarian becomes an executioner, at the request of his or her client. Please be sure that you could handle this infrequent yet very sad aspect of the veterinary profession.

One of the best ways to discern whether you are able to cope with the reality of unnecessary animal deaths is to volunteer at a clinic. Ask the veterinarian there if you could be present, whenever the client allows, during all or most of the procedures for putting animals to sleep. You may find that you can handle this experience from the beginning, or you may find that you could learn to accept it. But whatever you do, do not spend tens of thousands of dollars preparing for a profession from which you may turn away when you come to realize the number of clients who cannot afford procedures that you always believed were affordable and common. If you come from a middle-class or a wealthy family, you may be surprised how many clients ask to have their pets put to sleep. Do not be surprised. Try to gain some experience and see how often this happens.

A love of animals alone will not heal the animals that come to you. However, a love of animals, people, and science together will make you the best veterinarian that you can be.

Chapter One

About High School, College, and Veterinary School

Veterinarians undergo a significant amount of education before they earn their veterinary degrees. Before going to veterinary school, a typical pre-veterinary student completes four years of college (i.e., undergraduate) education. These four years are full of math and science. After four years of undergraduate study, another four years of veterinary school is required. Not all students are inclined to study for eight years after high school. For those who are not fond of college, a career as a veterinary technician may be more appropriate. This separate career will be discussed in Chapter Two.

Veterinary schools want their applicants to have successfully completed many different undergraduate science courses. To aid in the learning of this science material, most students find it helpful to take similar courses at the high school level.

The following is a list of college courses that are required of veterinarians. If you are not successful at completing these courses with good grades as an undergraduate, your chances of gaining admission to veterinary school would be greatly diminished.

Core College Prerequisite Courses

English Composition, full year
General Biology, full year with lab
General or Inorganic Chemistry, full year with lab
Organic Chemistry, full year with lab
Biochemistry, half year with lab, full year preferred
Physics, full year with lab
-These college courses are required by almost all U.S. veterinary schools.

If you skipped Biology, Chemistry, or Physics in high school, it would be difficult to succeed at these courses in college. College grades often make or break students' applications to veterinary school.

All of the science courses listed above should be taken for a full year with a laboratory component, except biochemistry, which is often a half-year course. These courses should *not* be taken on a pass/fail basis. Students should obtain a letter grade for each course as well as earn quality points for each subject.

In addition to the courses above, there are some additional courses that many American veterinary schools require as further prerequisites.

Strongly Recommended Prerequisite Courses
Genetics (23 of the 30 US veterinary schools require this course)
Microbiology (20)
Statistics or Mathematics (25)

Recommended Courses
Calculus (3)
Cellular Biology (6)
Nutrition or Animal Nutrition (8)
Physiology (6)
Oral Communications/Public Speaking (11)
Science electives or other science courses (11)

Additional humanities and social sciences courses are also almost always required. These courses are usually automatically met by following the general education requirements of any four-year degree program.

The decisions that you make about which courses to take should be dependent upon which veterinary schools to which you intend to apply for admission. For example, some of the courses listed above as 'recommended' are required at only a few veterinary schools. If you are not going to apply to any of those schools, then you may not want to crowd your undergraduate program with these courses. School-specific requirements may be found at PreVetAdvising.com and at aavmc.org.

<u>Why Is Math Required?</u>

There are many reasons that mathematics courses are required for applications to veterinary schools. As a veterinarian, you will prescribe drugs for the animals that you treat. One must mathematically formulate the amount of the doses of these drugs based on each animal's weight. A veterinarian must also be a good consumer of the statistical information that is released with the latest research in the field. Finally, understanding chemistry requires a good understanding of mathematics, particularly calculus.

Veterinarians use math every day. A veterinarian does not need to love math, but he or she must be able to do well in many different subjects of mathematics (including algebra, calculus, statistics, and trigonometry). The most important math course to take in high school is calculus. College chemistry requires a good understanding of calculus. If you purposefully skip high school calculus and/or pre-calculus, you may regret this decision during college as well as during your applications to veterinary school.

Plan Carefully

No matter how you go about deciding which courses to take, try to plan your program carefully. It is important to begin your first college term with Inorganic Chemistry and General Biology. These two courses are the cornerstones for the remainder of your education in science. A delay in beginning either of these courses in your freshman year may result in a fifth year in college.

> In veterinary school admissions selection processes, academic preparation always trumps animal and veterinary experience.

Veterinary school admissions offices look favorably on those applicants who are well educated in science and math. With a typical yearly class size of 100 students, a veterinary school usually has more than 800 applicants from which to choose. These schools can pick and choose whom they want, and they want applicants who have strong undergraduate programs and who have displayed excellent academic achievement. Good planning of your course of study will have a significant impact on your admission to veterinary school.

If you need help planning which college courses to take—and many students do—consider using the services of your college pre-health advisor or PreVetAdvising.com.

Academic Performance and Animal Experience

Many pre-veterinary students who have weak academic preparation believe that veterinary schools would look favorably upon them if their animal and veterinary experience is above average. Nothing could be further from the truth. In veterinary school admissions selection processes, academic preparation always trumps animal and veterinary experience.

I cannot stress this enough: It does not matter how well prepared you are when schools evaluate your animal husbandry skills; your academic preparation is much more important. If you have been successful in your academic preparation and the DVM admissions committee approves of this preparation, then your animal experience will be evaluated. If you have been unsuccessful in your academic preparation (e.g., poor grades and weak test scores), it is highly unlikely that the faculty would take the time to review your animal and veterinary experience. The review committee has too many applications to sort through, so its first elimination is usually decided by means of grades and admissions test scores.

Put yourself in their shoes. With so many students applying to veterinary school, why should veterinary schools take a risk on students with weak academic preparation? Veterinary schools do not want anyone failing out of their programs. Tough academic standards during the admissions process helps reduce the number of people who may drop out.

As a pre-veterinary advisor, this author cannot stress this point enough: You must display solid academic preparation and good grades to get into veterinary school. The following chapters will help you understand how to successfully prepare for the academic hurdles that you may experience on your long path to veterinary school.

Chapter Two

Advice for High School Students

E ven though veterinary school may be many years away, it is important to start planning your pre-veterinary years. There are some things that you can do in high school to make your college experience easier. As you prepare for college, do not only seek the advice of your high school college counselor; some counselors may not be aware of the competitive nature of veterinary school admissions. There are a few high school counselors who are not even aware that applicants need to attend college before beginning veterinary school. Your local veterinarian may be a good source of additional information and advice. In what follows, this author would like to discuss important topics on which you will need to make important decisions about your veterinary school preparation.

Chemistry, Calculus, and the Sciences

First and foremost, you should take Chemistry and Calculus. During your undergraduate program, you will take about three years of chemistry (Inorganic Chemistry, Organic Chemistry and Biochemistry) in order to qualify for admission at most veterinary schools. If you do not have high school chemistry under your belt, college chemistry courses would be much more difficult. Since college chemistry requires a good understanding of calculus (at some colleges it is required that you take calculus before beginning chemistry), you should also take high school calculus. If you feel that high school chemistry and calculus are too difficult, perhaps you should start thinking about another profession or career track – like that of a Veterinary Technician, which we will discuss soon. These courses will only become harder at the college level. Biology and physics are also required in college and should be taken first at the high school level.

Advanced Placement Credit

During high school, you may want to consider taking Advanced Placement (AP) courses. These are college-level courses that are taught for high school students. While certain veterinary schools have very strict rules about the acceptance of AP credits, you may, in general, use AP credits in order to skip the introductory-level courses that you would otherwise need to take as an undergraduate. For example, if you take AP Biology, you could skip Introductory Biology in college and enroll directly in a higher-level course. Remember, if you have taken AP Biology, you must have another biology course for admission to most veterinary schools. Higher-level courses, however, usually earn you more points during the DVM admissions process.

> First and foremost, you should take chemistry and calculus in high school.

Since AP credit policies differ among veterinary schools, and because school policies change from time to time, be sure to check out the AP policies in *Veterinary Medical School Admission Requirements* or at the different veterinary schools' websites. The VMSAR and school websites will have the best and most up-to-date information.

Some high school students take AP Chemistry and then begin their undergraduate program with Organic Chemistry. It is important to remember that some veterinary schools will not accept AP Chemistry. Additionally, because Organic Chemistry is so difficult, it may not be wise to begin this course without taking Inorganic Chemistry at the same college or university. We do not recommend taking AP Chemistry in High School. You may be better advised to take an AP humanities or social science course.

Three Years of Undergraduate College Education

It is possible to enroll in a DVM program after two or three years of college. Most veterinary schools allow applicants to enroll after applicants have completed three of their four years of undergraduate education. Some schools do not even require three years of undergraduate education. If you wish to be on the fast track into veterinary school, however, you must take Calculus and Chemistry in high school.

Pre-veterinary students who do very well in the first two years of college should think about applying at least one year earlier than typical pre-veterinary students. Doing well in your early years of college may save you a full year of tuition (and student loans)—perhaps even more. A good foundation in high school chemistry and calculus could help you to apply early and possibly save a year of tuition.

All Colleges Are Not Equal

Learn early on in your college search how to discern excellent colleges from good colleges. In your high school guidance office, you should find books like *Barron's Profiles of American Colleges* and *Peterson's Guide to Four-Year Colleges*. We recommend *Baron's Profiles of American Colleges* as it categorizes colleges in six categories of admissions selectivity whereas Peterson's uses only five categories. These books and their online resources categorize colleges into admissions selectivity groups. A college in which it is "Most Difficult" to gain admission is slightly better than a college that is "Very Difficult." Many college guides that are published today use different phrases, such as "Most Competitive" or "Highly Selective" when categorizing colleges. The language is not particularly important; it is the category or grouping of colleges that is important. If you attend a college that is "Less Competitive" (or "Less Selective"), you may harm your chances of gaining admission to veterinary school. Likewise, attending a college to which it is "Most Difficult" to gain admission may very likely increase your chances of admission.

The theory behind the importance of admissions selectivity is tied directly to the level of teaching at these colleges. Most good teachers teach to the middle of the class. In a college with an open admissions policy, you would find both very high-performing students and very low-performing students. The teachers at such a college will usually teach to the middle of this broad range. The teachers at a college such as Harvard, for example, teach to a very narrow range of high-performing students. The level of teaching is extremely high at universities like Harvard, while the level of teaching at community colleges, for example, is, by necessity, much lower. Community colleges serve a very important role in our higher education system, but they are not the best colleges to prepare students for long graduate or professional education.

With this said, it is important to recognize that there are many factors to consider when selecting a college. For example, let us assume that you have gained admission to a "Most Competitive" college as well as a "Very Competitive" college. Perhaps you like the "Very Competitive" college much more than you like the "Most Competitive" one. In the end, you should attend the college that feels best to you. The happier you are in college, the better chance you have of earning good grades. For this reason, admissions selectivity is only one factor among many to consider when choosing a college.

Beginning at a Two-Year College, Then Transferring

For both financial and other reasons, more and more students are deciding to begin their educations at two-year colleges with a plan to later transfer to a highly competitive four-year college. Many pre-veterinary students do exactly this and many are successful. However, transferring has some pitfalls.

The Cornell DVM Admissions Office analyzed a few years of admissions data and compared those students who attended both a two and a four-year college with those students who attended only one four-year college. We discovered that students who attended one college as opposed to two usually had higher grade point averages (GPAs). We concluded that many students do poorly in their first terms of college as they adjust to college life and to a new academic environment. This conclusion has been statistically validated by other researchers across many decades. Those students who had to adjust to two new colleges had, on average, two weaker terms of grades. This brought down their GPAs, and they had a more difficult time competing in DVM admissions processes.

Another issue with beginning your education at a two-year college and then transferring to a four-year one is the risk of changed sequences of chemistry material. Not all colleges teach this material in the same sequence. If you take inorganic chemistry at a two-year college and then take organic or biochemistry at a different college, the sequence of information may be different and you may do poorly in the latter two courses.

Science course grades are very important to DVM admissions, so you would want to be sure that each of your sciences, particularly the chemistries, have prepared you properly for the next level of courses. A professor at a four-year college will likely assume that you have had the course information presented to you in the same way that his or her college presents it. It is very difficult, indeed, almost impossible, for a professor to know the foundations of each student in his or her class.

When clients ask about beginning at a two-year college and then transferring to a four-year one, we almost always discourage this plan. There are times when it may be appropriate, however. If a student has doubts about his or her ability to do well in college and wants, at the very minimum, to earn a two-year degree, then a plan to transfer may be appropriate. Another scenario is when parents tell us, usually confidentially, that they believe that their child is not yet mature enough to live away from home. In this case, attending a community college may also appropriate. If a student is extremely shy, or has a difficult time making new friends, or perhaps has behavior problems or a chemical addiction that requires parental supervision, it may be appropriate that he or she begin education at the local community college.

If these words appear to contradict my previous claims about attending a highly selective four-year college, please realize that there are many shades of gray in our world. Everything is not black and white. Advising students and their parents is not easy, and there are exceptions to any point of view. For those students who know that they want to begin their educations at four-year colleges, the following may be helpful.

Our List of Recommended Pre-Veterinary Colleges

At the end of this book and at PreVetAdvising.com is a list of undergraduate colleges and universities that offer good pre-veterinary preparation. There are six criteria that an institution must meet in order to be listed. Briefly stated, a good pre-veterinary program must:

- Have an advisor who is a member of the National Association of Advisors for the Health Professions (NAAHP.org) or one of its regional associations.
- Have a vibrant pre-veterinary or pre-health club that is officially recognized by the student activities office or similar campus entity.
- Offer, on an annual basis, all of the basic science courses discussed in Chapter One.
- Offer Genetics, Microbiology, Statistics, and the courses listed on page 14 every other year, if not annually.
- Be a selective four-year college and offer a four-year degree in which all of the above mentioned courses apply toward that four-year degree.
- (Should) Maintain a list of veterinarians and organizations where pre-veterinary students may gain animal or veterinary experience.

Universities cannot purchase spots on our listing. Each college or university must meet these requirements and then apply to be listed on our website. Canadian and international undergraduate institutions are welcome to apply for inclusion in our list of recommended schools. The application is free.

If you do not see your college or university on our list of recommended colleges, this does not mean that your school is not a good choice. This institution may not be aware of our list and may not know to apply. There are, however, five questions that you can ask prospective colleges and universities to help you discern whether they offer a good pre-veterinary program.

Five Questions to Ask a Pre-Veterinary Program Director

Many colleges and universities recruit high school students who are interested in entering veterinary school. Many schools with formal pre-veterinary programs give their students an excellent preparation. Another subset of these schools does an adequate job of preparing future veterinary students and a third subset does a poor job. There is no accreditation system for pre-veterinary programs, so you are on your own in deciding whether a particular school would provide you with good pre-veterinary preparation. There are five good questions to ask when a college claims to have a pre-veterinary program.

The first question to ask is whether the director or other person within the pre-veterinary program is a member of the National Association of Advisors for the Health Professions or one of its regional associations (see NAAHP.org for links to the many regional NAAHP associations). If the program claims to prepare students for veterinary school yet no one on staff is a member of this pre-health advisors organization, you should be somewhat cautious. Likewise, if there is no pre-vet or pre-health program director, you should be cautious. You will need to seek constant advice from a pre-veterinary advisor during your four years of undergraduate study. If your advisor is not aware of the NAAHP or the program is too cheap to spend the money to belong to the NAAHP, then ask where the pre-veterinary advisor is getting his or her information about veterinary schools. One of the best and most efficient ways to receive this information is through the NAAHP or one of its regional associations. If the advisor receives all of his or her information from one veterinary school, the advice that you receive would probably be tailored to that school. You should make yourself eligible to apply to many veterinary schools, and your undergraduate program should help you do this.

The second question to ask is whether the pre-veterinary program facilitates shadowing experiences with local veterinarians. This may take the form of a simple list of local veterinarians who are willing to take on volunteers, or it may involve a more sophisticated list of internships and summer programs where you can gain animal and veterinary experience under a veterinarian who will later write a letter of evaluation for you. Every veterinary school either requires or strongly suggests a minimum of one letter from someone who can testify to your recent work with a veterinarian. It is common for veterinary schools to prefer two letters from veterinarians.

If you do not have experience that can be formally evaluated by one or more veterinarians, your chances of gaining admission would be greatly diminished. Ask the director, what help will the pre-veterinary program give you in arranging experience with a veterinarian either on- or off-campus? A pre-veterinary program does not need to have a veterinarian on staff in order to be a good program. However, the program should help you find experience where you are able to gain two to three hundred hours (or more) of experience that can be evaluated by a working veterinarian.

Please keep in mind that it is not necessary to attend a college with a pre-veterinary program. A pre-medical program provides virtually the same preparation. The difference between pre-medical and pre-veterinary preparation is whether or not you can gain animal experience with the help of your school. If you are on your own in arranging animal and veterinary experience, then you are in a pre-medical program, not a pre-veterinary program.

The third question to ask has to do with the courses that are offered in the pre-veterinary program or within the larger college or university. It is very uncommon for a pre-veterinary program not to offer the six basic courses that were discussed in Chapter One. If a pre-veterinary program does not offer these six courses annually, do not attend that institution. An easy way to check is to ask how often the school offers biochemistry. If it is not offered each year, red flags should fly. Since virtually

> There is no accreditation system specifically for pre-veterinary programs, so you are on your own in deciding whether a particular college will provide you with good pre-veterinary preparation.

all pre-veterinary programs do offer the basic courses, the more important questions to ask are: How many biological science courses are offered beyond the basic ones and how often are these courses offered? For example, a good number of veterinary schools require either Genetics or Microbiology or both. If one or both are offered every other year, this is probably sufficient, however you might encounter course scheduling problems.

If any of the courses listed in Chapter One are not offered every year or, at the least, every other year by the prospective college or university, you should probably not attend that school. Veterinary schools like to see a robust list of science courses on your transcript when you apply for admission. If you have difficulty scheduling courses due to the fact that these courses are not actually being taught on regular basis, the college is not giving you what you need. A good pre-veterinary program will consistently offer a wide variety of sciences annually.

The fourth question to ask is whether the college has an active pre-veterinary club or society. Almost all colleges have a pre-medical club or society, and you should have the resources of a student group that is focused specifically on veterinary school. If a college does not have a pre-veterinary club or society, it should not claim to have a strong pre-veterinary program. A pre-health club is very common, but in this admissions advisor's professional opinion, a pre-veterinary program should have a separate pre-veterinary club.

In our list of recommended colleges, we do include those institutions with only a vibrant pre-health club. If our list required institutions to also have a pre-veterinary club, only the largest universities would be included. There are many fine small colleges that we do not want to exclude. Many students prefer smaller institutions. In fact, for those students who have attended a smaller high school and had much interaction with their teachers, we recommend they attend a smaller college.

The fifth question—and most important question—to ask is how many pre-veterinary students have applied to veterinary schools and what is the success rate of these students in gaining admission to veterinary schools. If a college cannot provide you with a clear answer on this issue, be leery of attending this college. At the time that this book was first being published, less than one in two applicants gains admission to veterinary schools across North America. If the undergraduate college that you are considering has a 48% of its pre-veterinary students accepted to veterinary schools, they are on par with the better colleges. If a college has a significantly lower rate of acceptance, or if it cannot tell you its rate of acceptance, you may want to avoid that institution entirely.

It is also valuable if you are able to speak with a pre-veterinary student or two at that school, and before you visit a college you may wish to ask if this could be arranged. These students can tell you whether they are happy in their choice of college or whether they wish that they had attended a different pre-veterinary program.

If you discover that a college on our list of recommended undergraduate colleges no longer meets all of our requirements (if, for example, it does not have a pre-health advisor), please let us know as soon as possible at assistant@PreVetAdvising.com.

Location, Location, Location

Another consideration in choosing a college is location. When it comes to pre-vets, however, the concept of location has a twist. Most students grow up in urban or suburban environments. In Chapter Seven, we will discuss the importance of large animal experience. It is very beneficial to obtain both small and large animal experience before applying to veterinary schools. For this reason, you may want to select an undergraduate college that would make it easier for you to have access to large animals. A college near a racetrack or near dairy or other farms that have large animals may solve what many pre-veterinary students find to be a big problem—how to obtain large animal experience before applying to veterinary schools. Again, however, this is just one factor among many to consider when choosing a college. Colleges with Animal Science programs – usually located in suburbia or rurally – are an alternative we will discuss soon.

Veterinary Technology Programs

When selecting a college, some students consider studying veterinary technology at the undergraduate level. Veterinary technicians are aides to veterinarians, somewhat like nurses or physician assistants in human medicine. It is, however, a mistake to study veterinary technology in order to prepare for a medical education. Veterinary technicians learn routine procedures for nursing animals back to good health. They do not learn, as part of their core studies, all of the basic and strongly recommended science courses that were discussed in Chapter One. A pre-veterinary undergraduate program should be full of courses in math and basic science; anything that distracts students from math and science is likely, in the end, to harm one's chances of gaining admission to veterinary school.

Some veterinary technician programs have a pre-veterinary program built into the veterinary technician program. In most cases, these dual programs are fine as they should give you all of the same preparation in the basic sciences that other pre-veterinary programs give.

For those who do not want to attend the seven or eight years of college that it takes to become a veterinary doctor, there is a list of veterinary technology programs across the U.S. in Appendix Two. Veterinary technicians are in high demand across North America and this profession is a wonderful alternative for many students who may be thinking of a career with animals but who do not like the idea of eight long years of math and science.

Large or a Small College?

If you attended a large high school, you may be very comfortable attending a large university. If you attended a small high school and had significant interactions with your high school teachers, a large university may not be right for you. Large universities often have very large classrooms and class sizes. They often employ teaching assistants (graduate students who are working on their PhDs) who help the professor to teach classes of 200 or more students. If you are used to receiving direct help from your teachers, attending a large institution may be frustrating and even debilitating to your studies.

Further, teaching assistants can be helpful, but in the natural sciences many of the teaching assistants come from foreign countries and may not have a good command of the English language. Other teaching assistants may not be natural teachers.

When an institution publishes its student-to-faculty ratio, there are some caveats of which to be aware. First, not all faculty teach. At large research universities, the student-faculty ratio may look good on paper, but in actuality the number of faculty members who actually teach is often much smaller than is reported. Do not rely on the numbers published on a university's website. It is better to tour the campus and to ask your student tour guide how many students are actually in his or her classes. Do not ask for the student-faculty ratio or you will simply hear the party line. Try to ask about specific classes – particularly the sciences, the number of students in these classes, and the number of teaching assistants in each class. You may also want to ask the tour guide if he or she has had any professors or teaching assistants who did not have a good command of the English language. If the student says this has occurred, question yourself whether you want to be at a large university with a professor or TA you cannot easily understand.

Choosing a College with Unconventional Grading

The overwhelming majority of colleges and universities use a conventional grading system with grades of A, B, C, D, and F. Most use a standard 4.0 grading scale.

There are, however, a small number of colleges that offer narrative grades instead of conventional grades. Instead of giving students As, Bs, and Cs, the professor writes a short paragraph about the student's performance, and this paragraph appears on the student's transcript. Veterinary schools must compare apples to apples when they evaluate their applicants. Most veterinary schools will not accept narrative grades and will ask that each narrative grade be assigned a conventional grade that is officially approved by the institution's registrar's office.

If you attend a college that offers narrative grades and it cannot or will not convert these narrative grades into conventional grades, you would quickly and firmly close the door to most veterinary schools.

When a client asks about attending a school with a narrative grading system, we always recommend against doing so (and we usually cringe at the very thought of it). We do, however, make exceptions when the college records both narrative and conventional grades at the same time.

Some colleges that use narrative grading will promise a conversion at some point in the future. This usually requires the professor who first wrote the narrative to determine the student's conventional grade. Unfortunately, professors change jobs, leave institutions, retire, become ill, and even die. If a college does not record a conventional grade at the same moment that it records a narrative report, *do not attend that college*. There are many shades of gray in our world, but this is a clear-cut, black-and-white issue: You must have conventional grades in order to apply to most veterinary schools.

Choosing a College Major

Pre-veterinary students have some freedom to determine their majors. Theoretically, you could study any subject so long as you are able to take multiple science courses. In all practicality, however, veterinary schools require so many different sciences and mathematics courses that it is difficult to prepare for multiple veterinary schools if one is not a science major. Also, when admissions committees compare an applicant who is a science major with let's say marginal grades with an applicant who is, for example, a

> It is very beneficial to obtain both small and large animal experience before applying to veterinary schools. For this reason, you may want to select an undergraduate college that would give you access to large animals.

music major with marginal grades, the science major applicant is likely to be favored. Majoring in any science is a safer bet given the vast array of different science course requirements among the many different veterinary schools and the stiff competition for admission.

Still, it is not required that every pre-veterinary student become a science major. If you are unsure of your career path and you wish to explore many opportunities, a liberal arts major is probably the best choice. Please also keep in mind that more than half of those students who begin as pre-veterinary students end up pursuing different professions or career paths. Finally, there is no guarantee that you would complete a pre-veterinary program successfully. For example, many college students change their majors and career paths after receiving grades in Organic Chemistry. Organic Chemistry is not designed to be a 'wash-out' course, but so many students do poorly in Organic Chemistry that many find it unrealistic to enter in a highly competitive admissions process with the other applicants who did well in the course.

Do not be single-minded about choosing your major. Every pre-veterinary student should have a "Plan B," and your college major should open doors to this Plan B. Although we recommend any science major, we know that this is not the right course of action for every student. If your Plan B requires you to have a science background, then the decision of your major may be easier to make than it would be for someone who is considering two very different paths.

Very few people know at a young age where their lives will take them. Many college students change their majors and career paths at least once during college. Keep an open mind and consider all of your options when you choose your major.

Should You Choose an Animal Science Major?

Many high school counselors recommend that college-bound pre-veterinary students pursue programs in animal science. A good number of DVM applicants have academic backgrounds in animal science. There are many advantages to being an animal science major, but it is not necessary that you pursue this path. Most veterinary colleges want students with good foundations in basic science, and they want many different academic backgrounds represented in each new class.

Thinking more broadly, the profession also needs veterinarians who also have backgrounds in business, government relations, communications, marketing, leadership preparation, statistics, science research, and more. If everyone who applies to veterinary school had animal science backgrounds, the profession would suffer greatly.

If you feel that you may have difficulty gaining large animal experience before applying to veterinary college, attending a college with large animals on campus may be advantageous. Chapter Seven will address this issue and its importance. If you come from an urban environment and wish to attend college in an urban or suburban environment, you may not have easy access to large animals. Attending a college with an animal science program would likely provide you with some opportunities to work with large animals and to perhaps do so under a veterinarian. In Appendix Six, there is a list of colleges with animal science programs. Please keep in mind that they may not all have large animals on campus, so be sure to visit these colleges before selecting one for your studies.

Some people believe that there is one best path for pursuing a goal and that all other paths are either wrong or inferior. Some people see the world in black and white and have difficulty seeing its complexity. If your counselor does not present you with many paths or potential majors for pursuing admission to veterinary school, you may wish to find another counselor or mentor. Science teachers may have insights that they have drawn from their own college experiences. They may have had a college friend who pursued a pre-veterinary path in a unique way. Your local veterinarian may also have insight.

State or Provincial Residency

Another issue of location has to do with state or provincial residency. If you are from a state that does not have a veterinary school, you may want to consider establishing residency in a state that does have a veterinary school. Veterinary schools almost always give preference to students who reside in their own states. Some states allow you to establish residency during your undergraduate years. If your state does not have a veterinary school and does not have contracts with veterinary schools that give preference to home-state residents, then keep in mind what state residency you would possess at the time of your application to veterinary schools. Be aware as well that some states allow you to change your residency during your undergraduate studies. This may require you to become independent from your parents, which has income tax implications. We will further discuss residency issues in Chapter Eleven.

Letters of Evaluation

During high school, you may want to obtain some kind of formal animal experience. Formal animal experience includes any experience working with animals that is formally evaluated in writing by a veterinarian or other knowledgeable and objective person. While veterinary schools may want to see more recent animal experience than experience from your high school years, some schools may consider experience that was completed during high school as long as there is a corresponding letter of evaluation. Furthermore, obtaining some animal or veterinary experience with a written evaluation may open doors to other experiences later during college. When you approach future veterinarians for additional experience, having a letter of evaluation from a high school experience may be very useful to the future veterinarian. Many veterinarians have too many animal lovers wanting to volunteer; a letter of evaluation may help you gain a new experience within a different practice and with different species. Chapter Eight discusses letters of evaluation more thoroughly.

Chapter Three

Advice for College Students

The best predictor of future performance is past performance. This saying is true of professional athletes and of the financial industry as well as of academia. Admissions committees do not want to take the risk of admitting students with weak academic backgrounds. These committees always try to reduce the risk of admitting students who may later fail out of veterinary school, and they do this by admitting only those students who have displayed strong academic performance in the recent past.

It is important that pre-veterinary students understand this philosophy and strive for their academic achievements to be the best they can possibly be. Keep in mind during your college career this saying "the best predictor of future performance is past performance." This will be true of many of your endeavors, not just veterinary school admission.

College Course Load

Your course load is something over which you have control, and you would be wise not to take on too many courses at one time. This is especially true during the first term of your freshman year. Many students fumble in their coursework as they make the transition from home life to college life. Taking too many courses in your first term could set you up for failure.

As you progress through each term at college, you should slowly increase your course load. Veterinary schools like to see students who have taken heavy course loads. However, if you cannot earn high grades as you increase your course load, slow down and take as many courses as you can achieve at or above full-time status.

Full-time status is typically twelve credit hours at colleges on a semester system. Colleges on quarter systems have different definitions of full-time status. If there are multiple definitions of full-time status at any one college, use the definition that is employed by the financial aid office to distribute aid to full-time students.

Why follow the financial aid office's (FAO) definition of full-time status? FAOs must follow strict government guidelines when they distribute money to full-time students. If the FAO defines you as a full-time student and someone else is trying to convince you to take a heavier course load, just ignore that person or kindly point out the FAO definition of full-time status. Do not overload yourself, especially during your first term.

Virtually all graduate and professional school admissions officers see a very definite pattern of freshman not doing very well in their first term in college, only to improve later. This transitional term or year is usually the most difficult for students, and many freshmen who do poorly during this term may eventually realize that veterinary school is not in their future. We wish that we could speak with every college freshman or high school pre-veterinary student in order to give them a heads-up about the transitional term. Many fine students with great talent may not realize their dreams because they do not handle this transitional term well. Again, begin college with a minimum full-time course load and slowly increase this load above the minimum level. Veterinary schools eventually want to see a heavy course load before they admit you.

The Importance of Full-Time Status during Your Sciences

Veterinary school is a full-time endeavor. No one attends a DVM program on a part-time basis. The best predictor of future full-time academic performance in a rigorous science or veterinary program is past full-time academic performance with science coursework. Veterinary schools may not want risk to admitting students with science coursework that has been taken on a part-time basis. Further, do not try to load up on your coursework beyond what is necessary—especially during your first term. Again, the best predictor of future full-time academic performance in an intense science program is past full-time academic performance in a science program. Admissions officers everywhere recognize this. Eventually, juniors and seniors must demonstrate success in a heavier full-time course load. Be full-time your freshman year but do not take on more than the minimum full-time course load.

Grading Options

When planning your course load, you will also need to take into account different grading options from which you may be able to choose. Many students are tempted to choose a pass/fail grading option, and quite honestly, this option could make your courses a bit easier. To pass a course in this way, you usually need just the equivalent of a C grade. Veterinary schools do not want to see pass marks, however. They want to compare your A against Jenifer's B. Comparing one P to another P gives admissions committees no useful information to use when comparing students and selecting their classes. Comparing a P with a B, however, gives the student with the latter grade the upper hand in the selection process. For this reason, you should always take courses—especially math and science courses—with the conventional grading option. In some courses, such as Physical Education, colleges offer only pass-fail marks; but not to worry, admissions committees are usually aware of this regarding P.E.
Some colleges force all freshmen into pass/fail grading options. Some veterinary admissions faculty members may frown upon this

practice, but most understand the rationale. These colleges have acknowledged the well-proven fact that the freshman year is often students' worst in terms of grades, and they want their students to succeed. If you attend such a college, you may want to include a short note in your application that you were forced into a pass-fail grading system in your first year. You might also provide a URL to an official college website that describes this policy.

On the common (VMCAS) application for veterinary schools there is a section titled "Explanations." This section allows applicants to explain various situations that may not conform perfectly to a particular veterinary school's policies. It is important that you tell your admissions committees about those policies at your undergraduate institution that are different or unusual. Do not assume that all faculty members at all veterinary schools know all of the nuances in grading (and other policies) at every college in the country. It is simply impossible to understand all of these variations. The explanation section of the application is specifically designed for you to explain these nuances. You do not want to consume space in your personal statement/essay by explaining something important when there is an entire section in the application that is dedicated to such explanations. Please keep in mind, however: the explanation section is optional and should only be used when there is an unusual circumstance that is in need of explanation.

The Occasional Weak Grade

Hopefully, you would never come close to having a D, or worse, an F, on your transcript. However, if you feel that a bad grade is about to descend upon you, you should be aware that, in most colleges at least, you have the option of taking a W, or "withdraw." This W looks much better on your transcript than an F does. At some colleges, the W has been replaced by a WP (withdrew while passing) or a WF (withdrew while failing). If you feel that you may end up with a D or an F in a particular course, try to withdraw from the course while it is still possible to record a WP. Finally, any math or science course for which you have received a D, an F, or a W should be repeated or admission committees may have strong doubts about your ability. If you repeat any science or math course, repeat it during a full-time course load.

It is very important that you not have more than two Ws on your transcript. Admissions committees look at multiple Ws as an indication that you might withdraw from veterinary school. Again, past performance predicts future performance. Therefore, my suggestion above (to take a W instead of an F) comes with this caveat: do not do this more than once or twice. This also reinforces the first point of this chapter—do not overload yourself with work or you may have to withdraw once too often.

Multiple withdraw marks on a transcript indicate to admissions committees that a student has a history of quitting. The very last thing that admission committees want to risk is a withdrawal from veterinary school—or even from a single course. In veterinary school, if you do not complete all of your courses as they are offered, you must retake that entire year or semester of courses. Every seat in veterinary school is so expensive and so coveted that an empty seat in any required class represents a failure on the part of the admissions committee. In short, be careful about withdrawing from any course. If you have a W on your transcript, you should also have a reasonable explanation to include in your application to veterinary schools.

Most veterinary schools set the minimum acceptable grade in science and math courses at a C. In all honesty, however, these committees are hoping to see all A's and B's on students' transcripts, particularly in science courses.

The Sequence of Your Science Courses

Another important consideration in planning a successful academic program is the timing or sequence of your coursework. As a pre-veterinary student, you want to squeeze in every possible math and science course without overloading yourself. For this reason, it is important to begin the first term of your first year with General Biology and General/Inorganic Chemistry. All pre-veterinary students should take a three-year sequence of chemistry. These chemistry courses cannot be taken together, and they should be taken in this sequence:

> First, General/Inorganic Chemistry, a full year with lab
> Second, Organic Chemistry, a full year with lab
> Third, Biochemistry, a half year or more often with lab

If you begin Inorganic Chemistry in your sophomore year, you would then take Biochemistry in your senior year. If you fail or do poorly in any one of these chemistry courses and are forced to repeat a course, your three-year sequence then becomes a four-year sequence and you do not finish by your senior year. In fact, you would likely have to extend your undergraduate studies to a fifth year.

Likewise, General Biology should be taken during your freshman year because this opens the door to other coursework in the biological sciences. The later that you take General Biology, the later you are able to take biology electives such as Genetics and Microbiology. Since the admission requirements of veterinary schools differ greatly, and because it is advisable to apply to as many different veterinary schools as possible, every pre-veterinary student should make room in his or her program to take many different courses in the biological sciences. Starting early with General Biology is an obvious choice.

When you apply to veterinary school—which is most commonly done during your senior year—any prerequisites that you are taking in your senior year will not have a grade at the time of your application. Applying with any prerequisite course that does not yet have a grade could disadvantage you in comparison with other students who have completed all of their prerequisites by their junior years. Be sure to begin with Inorganic Chemistry and General Biology in your freshman year.

An ideal course schedule for pre-veterinary prerequisites usually looks like this:

> The best predictor of future academic performance is past academic performance.

Freshman Year
English Composition, a full year
General Inorganic Chemistry, a full year with lab
General Biology, a full year with lab
Calculus, if you did not take calculus in high school
A few courses in your major

Sophomore Year
Organic Chemistry, a full year with lab (a very difficult course)
Physics, a full year with lab
Statistics, one term
A few courses in your major

Junior Year
Biochemistry, at least one term, with lab if available
Genetics, one term with lab if available
Microbiology, one term with lab
Many courses in your major or other subjects

Senior Year
Two or three advanced biology's –based on the schools of your choice
Perhaps one math course –based on the schools of your choice
Many courses in your major or other subjects

Another issue in creating a good course schedule is planning for difficult courses. If there is a particular subject that you feel that you may do poorly in, do not plan to take another similarly difficult subject at the same time. We all have our favorite and less favorite subjects, and it is wise not to load up on these less favorite subjects during the same term.

One course that catches many pre-veterinary students by surprise is Organic Chemistry. Many students do so poorly in Organic Chemistry that they are forced to change their career paths and to turn away from veterinary medicine. Be particularly careful when you make your course selections during the year of Organic Chemistry. Also, we recommend that you buy your Organic Chemistry textbook a year early and study it during summer and other recesses.

Early Admission Programs

Many veterinary schools will accept college juniors before these students have completed their four-year programs. If you wish to apply early, it is essential that your chemistry and biology courses begin during the first week of college.

Some early admissions programs are designed to attract exceptional students before these students are eligible to apply to all veterinary schools. Other early admission programs are designed simply to reduce the usual eight years of undergraduate and graduate education to seven years, thus saving the DVM student one year of undergraduate tuition. The cost of DVM education is significant and starting salaries for DVMs may make it difficult for budding DVMs to live well and pay off their student debt at the same time. For these reasons, early admission programs should be investigated by anyone who is doing well in college and is trying to save on college tuition.

Veterinary schools may have special application procedures for their early admissions programs, so be sure to visit these schools' websites for early admission information.

Double Majors or a Major with a Minor Concentration

In a competitive admissions process, it is advantageous to have successfully managed a double major or a major with a minor concentration. Double majors and minor concentrations have their pitfalls because students sometimes over-commit themselves in the process. Since veterinary schools require so many math and science courses, the easiest double major or minor to attempt and meet veterinary school admissions requirements at the same time is a double major in two sciences, or one major in math and one in science. Again, this could give you an edge in the admissions process—but only if you do well in this more demanding course of study.

Get a Head-Start with Anatomy and Physiology

As you already know, veterinary schools require many different science courses. It is important to take Genetics and Microbiology because these are the most common science courses that are either required or preferred beyond the basic prerequisites of Biology, Chemistry, and Physics. If you have room in your program to take Human or Comparative Anatomy and Physiology, you would get a head-start on your first year of veterinary school.

We have already established that college freshmen are likely to earn weak grades as they transition from high school to college. The same is true for first-year DVM students. And what is usually taught at the very beginning of veterinary school? You guessed it: Anatomy and Physiology.

If a DVM student is going to fail a course, it is most likely to be their first one. Learning anatomy and physiology as an undergraduate would help you immensely in your first year of veterinary school. For many years, I asked first-year veterinary students at Cornell for one piece of advice that they might give to pre-veterinary students. Their answers were always the same: "Take Anatomy and Physiology."

If you do not have time for these courses, consider taking anatomy during the summer before veterinary school. It is unlikely that you would also be able to take Physiology during this same summer if it is taught separately from Anatomy. If you are admitted to veterinary school, it would not matter whether you took the course online or in a real classroom. The most important thing to learn about anatomy before veterinary school is its terminology. Otherwise you may find yourself in your first DVM class listening to a professor speak a foreign language. After all, most medical terms have their roots in Greek and Latin. If you know the terminology of your first course, you would be much more likely to succeed.

Many veterinary schools required Anatomy and Physiology years ago. When genetics, molecular biology, cell biology, and other newer material became more important, however, these schools moved away from this requirement. In my opinion, preparing for the first course of veterinary school is much more important than preparing for the newer sciences, which are taught later. After all, if you don't pass the first year of veterinary school, it won't be much help to have the newer sciences under your belt.

Summer Course Work

Many students plan to accomplish some coursework during a summer. There is nothing wrong with summer coursework as long as the course or courses that one takes are not science courses. Summer enrollment is usually part-time. Admissions committees want to see science courses completed during full-time enrollment because veterinary science courses are only given during full-time enrollment. No one has the option of being a part-time veterinary student. If you find that you need to complete summer coursework, take social sciences or humanities courses.

Also, please realize that summer courses are shorter in duration and therefore more material will be taught during each week when compared with fall or spring courses. Do not take a difficult subject during the summer— unless you know for certain that you will have plenty of time to do your homework during the compressed timeframe of the summer course.

Study Abroad

Many students desire to study abroad for one term of their college programs. Study abroad experiences look great on student transcripts because they indicate a willingness to learn outside of comfort zones. Indeed, the rigor of veterinary school is often outside the comfort zone of many DVM freshmen, so faculty members are likely to be impressed by your having lived abroad.

Despite these advantages, study abroad experiences must be timed well so as not to interfere with science prerequisites. You should not take core science prerequisites abroad as admissions committees may question whether these courses, taken in a foreign country, covered the same material that you would have learned in the United States or Canada. It is also best to avoid studying abroad during any year in which you have a yearlong sequence of a particular science course, such as Organic Chemistry. Generally speaking, yearlong science courses should be completed before your junior year, so planning a study abroad experience in your junior or senior year is usually a safe bet.

Be certain that your overseas coursework will appear, with a grade, on your home institution's transcript. If it does not, you may need to jump through an extra hoop during the DVM admissions process. Foreign transcripts usually require both an interpretation and an equivalency assessment. If the course appears on your home institution's transcript with a grade, no interpretation or equivalency would be needed.

We will soon discuss the many hoops that all applicants must jump through in order to meet basic application requirements. Applying is a long and tedious process; avoiding one small hoop could be very useful when you are trying to meet all of the other application requirements. For all of these reasons, do not enroll in core science prerequisite courses while studying overseas.

Extracurricular Commitments

Virtually all students have the desire to become involved in extracurricular activities. This is a normal and socially healthy desire. Indeed, veterinary schools look very favorably on extracurricular activities. Some students, however, become over-involved in activities, which drains time and energy away from their academic work. It is important not to get caught up in too many distractions and to leave enough time to be a good student. You have only one chance to earn good grades, but you will have many opportunities to become involved in activities both during and after college. Chapter Nine discusses this topic more thoroughly.

The Graduate Record Exam

One of the last efforts that you will make in preparation for your veterinary school admission is to prepare for the graduate admissions test, which is usually the Graduate Record Exam (GRE). You will want to set aside a good portion of time during the end of your junior year and the first term of your senior year, as well as the summer in between these years, in order to prepare for and take the GRE. Ideally, the test would be taken in June with an opportunity to repeat it in August, if needed. The GRE is more thoroughly discussed in Chapter Five.

The Unexpected Event

Sometimes unexpected scenarios occur during college. This is regrettable, but it is also a fact of life. There are three common scenarios (as well as numerous other scenarios) that may turn a student's world upside-down during college. These scenarios are usually out of one's control, and for this reason, this discussion might appear to be very pessimistic. I hope that none of these situations occur to you, although most graduate and professional school admissions veterans know that about 10% of all students will experience an unexpected event.

> The best predictor of future full-time academic performance in a rigorous science program is past full-time academic performance in a rigorous program with science coursework.

The three most common unexpected scenarios that have the potential to derail the academic progress of any fine college student are: a serious medical illness (most commonly, mononucleosis); the death of a loved one; and the divorce of parents back home. I have spoken with many students who have experienced one of these life-changing events, so it is with a deep heart that I write about these events. I have had students cry in my admissions office while relating their undergraduate hardships to me. On some occasions, I shed a tear with them.

Perfectly good students who make all the right decisions, work hard in college, earn fine grades, and gain the appropriate animal and veterinary experience have had their college experiences interrupted and sometimes completely derailed by unforeseen scenarios like the ones listed above. No one can help you to prepare for these scenarios. If you realize that you are in the middle of any one of these or any other unexpected scenario, please stop! It is perfectly acceptable to withdraw from one term of college when a major issue arises. It is not acceptable to withdraw here and there when a course becomes too difficult, but when you find yourself in a storm, take shelter. Admissions committees will understand this, especially if you adequately explain this serious life-changing event.

Since you may need to explain such an event, it is helpful to keep any documentation that you could possibly submit, or at least offer to submit, to veterinary school admissions offices. Admissions officers and faculty committees have been lied to many times. A doctor's written diagnosis, an obituary in a newspaper, or even divorce papers removes any doubt. By offering to submit documents or just submitting them without a request, you could provide admissions committees with the assurance that they are not being lied to.

Bad things happen in life, and these things could change your plans and academic progress. Be ready not just to recognize the existence of a life-changing event; be ready to take the appropriate steps to handle your medical or emotional health.

Pausing your studies, saving documents that may seem meaningless to keep at the time, and knowing when to take shelter, so to speak, could make a big difference. If you find yourself in a storm and are unsure what to do, visit your pre-health advisor or contact PreVetAdvising.com for an appointment. If you seek our advice during our busy season and we are backlogged, be sure to tell us that you need an appointment quickly.

I sincerely hope that your life in college is not interrupted by a major unanticipated or difficult event. If it is interrupted, however, be prepared to quickly recognize this fact and respond appropriately.

Chapter Four

Advice for Returning Adult Students

The returning adult student, or non-traditional student, is someone who returns to college after having been in the workforce. Many returning adult students are doubtful that they have a real chance of successfully competing with students fresh out of college. The answer is that they really do have good chances and that there are many returning adult students who are currently enrolled in veterinary school.

Indeed, much of the advice below for non-traditional students is similar to the advice given above for younger students. Before reading this chapter, returning adult students should also read Chapters One and Three as virtually all of the advice in those chapters apply to them as well.

First, Take the GRE®

If, as a returning adult student, you have three to four years of college education behind you, the very first thing that you want to do is take the Graduate Record Exam on an unofficial basis and obtain an unofficial score. If this score is too low, then you would want to work hard on improving it. In the unlikely event that your practice score does not improve, you may really want to consider whether or not to pursue veterinary school admissions. The next chapter includes tables that indicate desirable GRE scores levels in relation to GPA levels. It should be noted that students who take practice GRE tests repeatedly often increase their GRE scores. Do not give up after one or two practice tests. Keep practicing. The more you become familiar with any standardized test, the better you would do on the real thing.

After you have completed a GRE self-assessment (using the software and preparation books that are available in most bookstores) and you are satisfied with your GRE scores, it is time to begin the coursework that all students must complete as part of any pre-veterinary program. Every returning adult student begins from a different starting line when he or she addresses prerequisites. Some returning students have chemistry backgrounds, and others do not. The first prerequisites with which any returning adult student should be concerned are the chemistries because, as the previous chapters discussed, they involve a three-year sequence.

The best advice is always individually tailored, however, and it is strongly recommended that you seek out your pre-veterinary advisor or visit PreVetAdvising.com in order to arrange a free appointment.

The Importance of Full-Time Status

For the same reasons discussed in the previous chapter, you should always take your science courses on a full-time basis. You will be competing with applicants who completed their coursework while they had full-time status, and they would likely have the upper hand when compared with others who have only part-time science coursework. In many cases, this means that the returning adult student must quit his or her job in order to prepare for admission. Being part-time is a sure way to diminish your chances of admissions.

There are exceptions to this rule of thumb, of course. Returning adult students who have taken full-time science course loads in the past and earned high grades do not need to do more science coursework on a full-time basis. Again, a pre-veterinary advisor may help you with these decisions. As always, the best predictor of future full-time academic performance in the sciences is past full-time academic performance in the sciences.

Repeating Old College Courses

Many CVM admissions offices have a five- or ten-year limit on how long ago a particular college course may be completed. Let us assume for a moment that a returning adult student has previously taken the chemistry sequence, but that he or she is wondering whether these courses need to be taken again so the content is current and up-to-date. If a returning student's chemistry grades were good, it is recommended that he or she retake only Biochemistry. Biochemistry is the capstone of the chemistries, and retaking only that chemistry should be sufficient. However, because many veterinary schools have limits on how old courses can be at the time of application, it is also advisable to retake whatever courses the veterinary school to which you are applying requires, if only to be more current. Check first with the veterinary school in your home state and then with other schools of your preference about their time limits.

Now let us assume a different situation. Perhaps a returning adult student took only Inorganic Chemistry and earned a C. Since Organic Chemistry is a big 'wash-out' course, it is strongly advised that this student repeat Inorganic Chemistry before taking Organic Chemistry. If the lab grade for the former course was a B or better, one option is to retake Inorganic Chemistry part-time through an online course. You may be scratching your head, wondering why I'm recommending part-time science coursework. In this particular situation, however, the student would be retaking the lecture part of Inorganic Chemistry solely to help him or herself prepare for Organic Chemistry. When you take Organic Chemistry, you want to be full-time.

Do not repeat any coursework in the biological sciences (except for required courses in which you have a D). There are plenty of new or other courses, like Genetics, Cell Biology, and Molecular Biology, in which you can earn good grades. These courses would also provide you with new knowledge that is relevant to any medical education. Retaking a basic science course instead would simply distract you from learning new material. A quick rule of thumb is that it is always better to learn new material rather than repeat old material. Of course, if your veterinary school(s) requires a higher grade than the one you initially received, then you must repeat the old material. If they accept your original grade, however, move on to new knowledge and earn good grades while learning this new material.

Returning adult students face many variables, so it is best to seek out a pre-veterinary advisor on campus. Many returning adult students are not well connected to their pre-health advisor. This occurs for a variety of reasons. Most returning adult students take their courses in the evening or on weekends when the pre-health advisor is typically unavailable. Contact him or her and ask if you could arrange an appointment outside of normal business hours. If they cannot accommodate you, our service is available to fill in these gaps. Do not proceed with your preparation if you lack good information. The information is out there, and we could help you to find and process it.

Do Not Attend a Two-Year College

As was discussed in Chapter Two, attending a less rigorous college would not help you to gain admission to veterinary schools. Try to attend a highly selective four-year college in order to complete any science prerequisites. If you did not read the section in Chapter Two about the importance of attending a selective institution, please go back and read that section.

It is also important to keep the number of colleges you attend to a minimum. When admissions committees see science coursework taken at many different institutions, they sometimes have an uneasy feeling about the applicant's science preparation. Again, many sciences require good foundations in basic science and jumping from one college to another does not do the applicant, or his or her education, any favors. In short, attend a minimum of highly selective colleges.

Distance Education and CLEP®

Many students ask whether distance education via the internet or CLEP (College Level Examination Program) tests may be used in order to satisfy pre-veterinary science prerequisites. The answer is usually no. Veterinary schools want to see laboratory work attached to science coursework, and distance education and CLEP do not provide adequate, if any, lab work. Therefore, it is best to take science courses the old-fashioned way— on campus and in a real classroom and laboratory. If you wish to take a science course that does not have a laboratory requirement, you can check with your preferred veterinary schools and their offices of admission about taking a science course outside of a traditional classroom.

If you want to take some courses by means of distance education or CLEP, we recommend that you take social sciences or humanities classes. Please remember that to be acceptable all courses must appear on an official college transcript from an accredited college. Some online schools do not have proper accreditation. Be sure that your online school does have proper accreditation. You could do this by asking the admissions office or the registrar of that school to provide you with documentation.

There is one last point about distance learning which involves financial aid. Your home college would most likely not provide you with financial aid to attend another college, and online colleges do not give financial aid to students who are less than half-time. If you are dependent on financial aid to finance college, distance learning is not always the most affordable option. Some veterinary schools require an animal nutrition course, which can only be found at large universities. If you attend a small college, you may need to take this course online from a large university, and probably with no financial aid for this course. It is very sad that some veterinary schools are deliberately increasing the cost of an undergraduate education by requiring hard-to-find courses.

Verify Whether a College is Truly Accredited

The best way for a U.S. student to check on accreditation is to perform a free online search at the U.S. Department of Education's database of accredited institutions. This database is available at:
http://ope.ed.gov/accreditation/Search.aspx

Be sure to know which agency is accrediting your program and to check the above website in order to confirm that this body is recognized by the U.S. Department of Education. If your program is not accredited by a federal government approved accrediting body, either question your school about this fact or simply move on to a different college that is accredited.

Post-Baccalaureate Degree Programs

Many returning adult students ask whether a degree program is appropriate for completing their science coursework. If you already have a four-year degree, another degree is usually unnecessary, and you may take science courses as a non-matriculated (non-degree) student. However, as a non-matriculated student, you may have a difficult time getting access to these courses. Most colleges have non-matriculants register last, at which point many classes have full enrollment. One way of avoiding this problem is to enroll in a pre-medical post-baccalaureate program. There are websites dedicated to listing and describing these programs.

Before enrolling in a post-baccalaureate program, you should visit the colleges to which you are considering applying and ask whether or not it is necessary to be matriculated in order to gain access to the proper courses. Attending a post-baccalaureate program is only necessary if it is the only sure way to enroll in the courses that you need.

The following is a partial list of institutions offering post-baccalaureate programs for pre-medical/pre-veterinary preparation.

Auburn University	Auburn University, Alabama
Boston University	Boston, Massachusetts
Brown University	Providence, Rhode Island
Case Western Reserve University	Cleveland, Ohio
Columbia University	New York, New York
Cornell University	Ithaca, New York
Duke University	Durham, North Carolina
Emory University	Atlanta, Georgia
Florida State University	Tallahassee, Florida
George Washington University	Washington, District of Columbia
Georgetown University	Washington, District of Columbia
Harvard University	Cambridge, Massachusetts
Howard University	Washington, District of Columbia
Iowa State University	Ames, Iowa
Johns Hopkins University	Baltimore, Maryland
Kansas State University	Manhattan, Kansas
Louisiana State University	Baton Rouge, Louisiana
Loyola University Chicago	Chicago, Illinois
Marquette University	Milwaukee, Wisconsin
Michigan State University	East Lansing, Michigan
Mississippi State University	Mississippi State, Mississippi
New York University	New York, New York
Northwestern University	Evanston, Illinois
Ohio State University	Columbus, Ohio
Oklahoma State University	Stillwater, Oklahoma
Oregon State University	Corvallis, Oregon
Purdue University	West Lafayette, Indiana
Saint Louis University	Saint Louis, Missouri
Southern Illinois U. Carbondale	Carbondale, Illinois
Stanford University	Stanford, California
Stony Brook University	Stony Brook, New York
Syracuse University	Syracuse, New York
Temple University	Philadelphia, Pennsylvania
Texas A & M University	College Station, Texas
The University of Tennessee	Knoxville, Tennessee
Tufts University	Medford, Massachusetts
Tulane University of Louisiana	New Orleans, Louisiana
University at Buffalo	Buffalo, New York
University of Arizona	Tucson, Arizona
University of California-Davis	Davis, California
University of California-Irvine	Irvine, California

University of California-UCLA	Los Angeles, California
University of California-San Diego	La Jolla, California
University of Chicago	Chicago, Illinois
University of Cincinnati	Cincinnati, Ohio
University of Connecticut	Storrs, Connecticut
University of Florida	Gainesville, Florida
University of Georgia	Athens, Georgia
University of Hawaii at Manoa	Honolulu, Hawaii
University of Illinois at Chicago	Chicago, Illinois

There are many other lists available on the internet. Perhaps one of the best listings of pre-medical/veterinary post-bac programs is at the American Association of Medical Colleges at services.aamc.org/postbac/index.cfm.

Your Personal Statement

The personal statement (referred to here as your essay) is very important to your DVM admissions success. Every older student has a unique story to tell about his or her road to veterinary school. Use this opportunity to effectively tell your story. Faculty members become bored reading countless similar essays, and returning adult students' essays usually involve unique stories about how these students have turned their sights on veterinary medicine. Most returning adult students are able to say things that most traditional students cannot. You have life-experience beyond what the typical college student has. Talk about this life experience. You might begin your essay by saying that you have been in the workforce and have overcome some (or many!) obstacles in the working world and that this has made you stronger. We will discuss essays later in this book.

Diversify Your Animal & Veterinary Experience

One advantage that returning adult students usually have is that they have had more time to gain animal and veterinary experience. It is impossible to overstate the importance of diversifying your experience with animals. Many undergraduates become too focused on a particular aspect of veterinary medicine and fail to diversify their animal and veterinary experience. You can give yourself a unique advantage by not making the common mistake that too many undergraduates make.

You have experienced the real world and you know to keep your eyes open and to consider new opportunities. You would not be changing careers if your eyes were closed to the world's many possibilities. Use this advantage to obtain plenty of diverse experiences with animals. Remember, do not gain too much experience with small animals at the expense of gaining a balance of experience with large animals and other species.

Begin a VMCAS Application—For the Sake of Familiarization

The Veterinary Medical College Application Service's (VMCAS) online forms are available only from June to September 15. It is a good idea for all prospective applicants to look at the form and its numerous questions. Appendix Four of this book includes descriptions of the types of questions that you will be asked. However, it does not include the pull-down menus and other detailed information with which you may want to become familiar. If you are a year or more away from applying, go online (June – September 15) and take a look at everything that will be asked of you later on in the process. Setting up a VMCAS account does not obligate you to submit an application.

> Every older student has a unique story to tell about their path to veterinary school.

There is also an application sample that includes an outline of the VMCAS questions, and this is available year-round. However, the application sample does not allow you to see the various pull-down menus and the actual plurality of questions regarding your coursework and grades that will appear on the real application. Completing an actual application without submitting it would give you a better sense of the amount of time you would need to complete the actual application.

Do Not Become Discouraged

Many returning adult students struggle with the preparation for veterinary school. Often, they must balance employment, families, and animal and veterinary experience in addition to their coursework. It is very easy to become overwhelmed by this experience. You should know that this new workload is actually good experience for veterinary school. Any medical education is overwhelming. There is so much knew knowledge to cram into existing medical programs, and faculty and students alike often feel overwhelmed.

Second, your real world experience accounts for a lot in the admissions process. All committees wonder whether the students who they are about to admit are mature enough for a tough four years of veterinary school. They do not want anyone to withdraw for any reason and they want to see their students succeed.

Returning adult students are much safer bets by admissions committees when the maturity factor is considered. In fact, a small number of my clients who applied straight out of college were not accepted at first. It was only after a few years in the real world that they had better applications. These students were able to entertain multiple offers after a few years of real world experience. Returning adult students should keep this positive aspect of their applications in mind and use it to their advantage.

A Recap for Returning Adult Students

Let's quickly recap the points made for the returning adult student:

1. Practice the GRE and be able to achieve a good score (65th percentile or more) before taking too many pre-veterinary courses.

2. Begin the chemistry sequence early, especially if you did not have a lot of chemistry in your undergraduate program.

3. Repeat only those courses that you must repeat. If possible, avoid repeats and learn new material.

4. Try to arrange full-time studying of your sciences.

5. Make the most of your essay. If possible, explain how your life experience has challenged you and made you stronger.

6. Diversify your animal and veterinary experience.

7. Go online to VMCAS one year before applying in order to look through the very long application. Do not submit this trial application; just become familiar with it.

8. Do not get discouraged. Seek help whenever you feel that you need it. Don't go it alone!

> First, take a practice GRE test. If you like your practice score, then begin the three-year chemistry sequence. Do not enroll in many pre-requisites if you are not confident you will do well on the GRE.

Chapter Five

Admissions Tests: The GRE and the MCAT

Almost all veterinary schools in North America require or accept the Graduate Record Exam (GRE®). Some allow the Medical College Admissions Test (MCAT®) instead of the GRE. The GRE is the test that will open the most doors to veterinary admissions and it will therefore receive more attention in this chapter. In addition, the GRE will give you the option to apply to other graduate schools if you do not gain admission to veterinary school.

Prepare on Your Own for the GRE

The GRE is very similar to the Scholastic Aptitude Test (SAT®), which is the test most commonly required at the undergraduate level on the east coast. The Educational Testing Service (ETS®) produces both tests. To help prepare students for the SAT, ETS developed the Preliminary SAT or PSAT®. Unfortunately, there is no preliminary GRE. Therefore, it is the responsibility of each student to prepare for the GRE on his or her own. Most bookstores have a section of books and software that include college admissions preparation material. Preparing on your own will often marginally increase your GRE scores. Practicing the test would prepare you for the type of questions that you will see on the official test. Since the GRE is a computer-based test, you would want to eventually buy computer-based practice software. There is also free practice software at GRE.org.

While many companies produce and sell test preparation software, the best software is produced and sold by the GRE organization itself. Other companies cannot possibly know the GRE as well as the people who design and produce the actual test. In August 2011, a newly revised GRE test was introduced. Other companies made immediate claims that their software would prepare you for this new test. How could that be? These other companies were not given information on the test by the company that designs the GRE. These companies have to purchase the GRE software in order to make their own software. Although GRE-produced software may be a little pricey, it is worth spending the extra money for a product that has insider information about the test.

While in college, you should check with your pre-health advisor about free, college-based GRE preparation courses. The GRE does not offer such courses while The Princeton Review and Kaplan (to name only two) do. First, inquire about the free courses that may be offered by your college or university. If your institution does not offer a free or low-cost course, then consider those vendors that do.

Many veterinary schools put equal weight on the GRE and GPA. For these schools, the lower your GPA, the higher your GRE should be and vice versa. It is difficult to estimate which combinations of GPA and GRE score levels work well in the admissions process, but below are charts that have been created from three decades of admissions experience.

There are three sections to the general GRE – as opposed to the company's subject tests, which are not your concern. These are the verbal subtest, the quantitative subtest, and the analytical writing subtest. The GRE percentiles below are an average of the percentiles of the verbal and quantitative subtests. Many veterinary schools do not require the third subtest –analytical writing subtest. In no way do the following numbers guarantee your admission to a veterinary school. These are estimates only of which GRE percentile you want with a given GPA. Since most colleges have a maximum GPA of 4.0, this chart is written using that common scale. Obviously, the best combination of GPA and GRE scores would be a 4.0 GPA and the 99% on the GRE tests.

Table 2: GPA and Percentiles of Achievement on the GRE

Minimum Test Score Levels		Favorable Test Score Levels	
GPA	GRE%	GPA	GRE%
4.0	50	4.0	74
3.9	55	3.9	77
3.8	60	3.8	80
3.7	63	3.7	83
3.6	66	3.6	86
3.5	69	3.5	89
3.4	72	3.4	92
3.3	75	3.3	95
3.2	80	3.2	97
3.1	85	3.1	98
3.0	90%	3.0	99%

Do not let these numbers scare you away from applying to veterinary school. Each veterinary school has a different set of admissions policies, and you would not know whether or not you are admissible unless you apply. If you score low on the GRE and you are afraid that you would not gain admission because of it, there are some things that you can do to help your chances. One common piece of advice given to clients is to practice the test—with the available software—three or four times in order to become familiar with the test and to reduce the chances of any surprises during the official test.

By the way, many teachers, counselors, parents and students focus on the raw score as opposed to the percentile of achievement for each test. Raw scores are just that – raw. By converting the raw score into a percentile, the test giver distributes a more accurate score. Since the GRE test actually changes slightly every month, a raw score on two different months may not be completely equal to each other. ETS knows how to provide a better score and they do so when they give the percentile. Many colleges and universities use the raw score to compare students when ETS has been saying for decades to use the percentile. It is unclear to this author why they even bother distributing the raw score. So it is most important that you focus on your percentile of achievement than on the raw score.

When you actually take the official computer-based test, you will receive your raw scores at the end of the test session. You will then know if you need to schedule another test. The percentiles of achievement will be sent at a later date, after all administrations of the test for the given month are completed and scored.

If you are unhappy with the results of your own preparation for the GRE, you may want to consider preparatory courses. These courses are given by a number of private vendors. Private courses can be pricey, but they could often make a difference. The best advice, however, is to prepare on your own before you spend your good money on a preparation course.

Preparing for the GRE Verbal Subtest

There is a little known secret about preparing for any verbal test, and you can use this to your advantage. Larger universities usually offer an English course on the Greek and Latin roots of the English language, often titled Etymology. Consider taking this course to expand your vocabulary. Most verbal tests, including the GRE verbal subtest, are in large part tests of vocabulary. If a test-taker has a broad vocabulary or, more importantly, knows how to decipher words that he or she may never have learned, that test-taker would have an advantage over other people who cannot decipher words. Furthermore, medical terminology is largely based on these languages. Etymology is a very useful course for any pre-health student.

You do not need to attend a large university in order to find a course on the Greek and Latin roots of the English language. Search the internet for the phrase "Greek and Latin roots of English" or for "Etymology." If you dig deep enough, you will find some institutions that teach this course through distance learning. If your practice verbal score on the GRE is below the 70th percentile, it would be worth investing both the time and the money to learn the Greek and Latin roots of English. Since this course is not required by veterinary schools, you may audit it if you prefer.

A course in medical terminology may also provide you with similar information but may not prepare you for the GRE as well as a course in Etymology may do so. Likewise, learning anatomy and physiology would, as discussed earlier, expose you to terms used in those courses at veterinary colleges, but would not best prepare you for a standardize verbal test. Again, if you do not understand the vocabulary on a verbal test, you would likely not do well on that test. Verbal tests are, in large part, a vocabulary test. Do all you can do to improve your vocabulary before sitting for any verbal standardized test.

Table 3a: Admissions Tests & Past Deadlines

U.S. Veterinary Colleges at	Scores Received[1]	Acceptable Test(s)
Auburn University	1-Sept	GRE
University of California, Davis	15-Sept	GRE
Colorado State University	15-Sept	GRE
Cornell University	30-Oct	GRE or MCAT
University of Florida	31-Aug	GRE
University of Georgia	15-Sept	GRE
University of Illinois	1-Oct	GRE
Iowa State University	15-Sept	GRE
Kansas State University	15-Sept	GRE
Lincoln Memorial University	30-Sept	GRE
Louisiana State University	1-Oct	GRE
Michigan State University	30-Sept	GRE
Midwestern University	15-Aug	GRE
University of Minnesota	15-Sept	GRE
Mississippi State University	1-Oct	GRE
University of Missouri	15-Sept	GRE or MCAT
North Carolina State University	15-Sept	GRE
Ohio State University	30-Sept	GRE or MCAT
Oklahoma State University	1-Nov	GRE
Oregon State University	15-Sept	GRE
University of Pennsylvania	1-Oct	GRE
Purdue University	15-Sept	GRE
University of Tennessee	15-Sept	GRE
Texas A. & M. University	1-Oct	GRE
Tufts University	15-Sept	GRE
Tuskegee University	1-Oct	GRE
Virginia-Maryland Regional	15-Oct	GRE
Washington State University	15-Sept	GRE
Western U. of Health Sciences	15-Sept	GRE or MCAT
University of Wisconsin	1-Oct	GRE

Canada		
University of Calgary (Alberta)		
Guelph University (Ontario)		
Univ. of Montreal (Quebec)		Fluency in French[5]
Prince Edward Island University		GRE
Saskatchewan University		

Table 3b: Admissions Tests & Past Deadlines
(Most International CVMs do not readily provide test deadlines.)

Central America		Scores Rec'd[3]	Notes
Cayman Island	St. Matthew's University		GRE Recommended
Costa Rica	Universidad VERITAS		Fluency in Spanish[5]
Grenada	St. George's University		GRE or MCAT
Mexico	National Autonomous U. Mexico		Fluency in Spanish[5]
St. Kitts	Ross University		GRE

Europe			
Denmark	University of Copenhagen		Fluency in Danish[5]
Ireland	Dublin U. College		
Netherlands	Utrecht University		Fluency in Dutch[5]
UK Scotland	University of Edinburgh	1-Oct	GRE
UK Scotland	University of Glasgow		May review GRE
UK England	University of London		

Pacific			
Australia	Melbourne University		
Australia	Murdoch University		
Australia	University of Queensland		
Australia	University of Sydney		GRE or ISAT
Japan	University of Tokyo		Fluent in Japanese[5]
New Zealand	Massey University	1-Nov	GRE (Americans)
Philippines	Central Luzon State Univ.		
South Korea	Seoul National University		

Important notes:
1. Most veterinary schools set a date by which they must receive scores. Many also have an examination deadline. It is sometime unclear which date they intend to publish.
2. Some schools allow unofficial data by the deadline; others do not.
3. Some CVMs publish no date or requirement.
4. The GRE may take up to 30 days after the exam to deliver your scores. It's advisable to sit for your first GRE by June 30.
5. You must be very fluent in the language of instruction. To attend a foreign veterinary school, you must be able to understand complex terminology in the language of instruction. Your fluency in everyday conversation is not a good predictor of how you might learn medical terminology in a foreign language. A medical education in a foreign language may be academic suicide for some.

Sources: AAVMC and CVM websites

Test Score Deadlines

As Table 3 shows, veterinary schools have different deadlines for submitting standardized test scores. Please keep in mind that for those schools that have a September 15 test deadline, this date may change if the normal VMCAS application deadline of September 15 falls on a weekend.

You may sit for the GRE once every sixty days. Since many students do not like their first test scores, it is important to schedule your first test for June or early July. If you feel the need to retake the test, you would then have time for a second test in August or September. After September, many veterinary schools will not accept scores for the application cycle then in progress. For applications to most veterinary schools, scores earned after September would not be useful until the following application cycle, which begins almost a year later.

The MCAT

The Medical College Admissions Test is accepted at five veterinary schools, all of which allow you to submit either GRE or MCAT scores. These five veterinary schools are located at Cornell University, University of Missouri, The Ohio State University, Saint George's University, and Western University of the Health Sciences. A good score on the MCAT is a 32 or 33 out of 45 total points.

> Knowing the Greek and Latin roots of the English language not only helps you on any verbal test, it will help you during your entire medical education.

Like the GRE, there is no preliminary MCAT from which you can prepare for the real test. So again, it is in your best interest to prepare on your own using study guides and software before taking the official MCAT test. You can purchase preparation material at the MCAT website.

The Fairness of Standardized Testing

Some students resent any form of standardized testing. However, in order to become a licensed veterinarian one must first pass a licensing exam. This too is a standardized test. The North American Veterinary Licensing Exam (NAVLE) is required of all DVM licensees in all states, and it is one important reason that veterinary schools require a standardized test for admission. These schools want to know that you can perform well on a standardized test for both admissions and licensing purposes.

Those who do not try to speak formal English in their home, and wish to attend a university in which the language of instruction will be mostly formal English, they will be at a disadvantage. Any standardized test written in a language (with proper language constructs) will disadvantage those who do not have a firm, everyday, grasp of that language. American parents who do not correct poor English spoken in the home or do not encourage English to be spoken in the home are not doing their children a favor, especially if they want their children to attend an English-speaking university.

There may be culturally bias questions within American standardized testing, yet it is this educator's belief that poor performance on standardized tests by certain ethnic groups is generally more a function of a poor understanding of proper English than it is of, for example, culturally bias questions. Test designers must be careful to avoid culturally bias questions, but test takers, and their parents, should also take responsibility for learning and speaking proper English. Using sloppy English regularly "ain't going to get you nowhere!"

As mentioned earlier, some students do not perform well on standardized tests, regardless of their English proficiency. If you are one of these students, there are many English-speaking, accredited veterinary schools that do not require any test, both in Canada and overseas. Since you will still need to pass a standardized test for licensing purposes, it is recommended that you keep trying to do well on standardized tests. For admissions purposes, however, you have options to apply to schools that will not require test scores.

The Veterinary College Admissions Test

The Veterinary College Admissions Test (VCAT®) was a standardized test that was accepted by a handful of veterinary schools. It was discontinued in 2004. References to the VCAT can still be found on out-of-date websites. If you come across any of these references, just ignore them as the VCAT is no longer offered. References to the VCAT is a good indication that any website referring to the VCAT is unreliable.

Chapter Six

Advice for International Students

Canadian students are considered to be international students when they apply to U.S. veterinary schools. The same is true of American students who apply to Canadian schools. This section is written primarily for international students who wish to apply to U.S. veterinary schools. It is especially written for those international students who do not speak English as their first, primary language.

There are two substantial questions that veterinary schools ask of international students when they apply to American educational programs: Is the student proficient in the English language and can he/she afford an American education? Of course, when English is the first official language of your country, language proficiency is usually not an issue. However, students from French-speaking Quebec, for example, may need to provide evidence of their English proficiency.

English Proficiency

When you attend any medical or veterinary school, you will learn a new language of medical terms that are mostly Greek and Latin in origin. All medical schools, including veterinary medical schools, use these terms in virtually every class. If you are not highly proficient in the English language, it will be almost impossible to learn this medical language when it is taught in formal English. You must convince admission committees that you can do well on English language tests such as the GRE verbal subtest and the Test of English as a Foreign Language (TOEFL®). It is also best to convince these committees that you are fluent in both formal and conversational English.

If you are not highly proficient in the English language or cannot speak conversational English with ease, then you should not consider applying to English-speaking veterinary schools. It may be beneficial to attend an American undergraduate college for one year instead and earn grades in science courses that are taught in English. In fact, many U.S. veterinary schools require this of international students (i.e., one year of college in an undergraduate college program that is taught in English).

Please keep in mind that some veterinary schools do not accept any international students. This may be attributable to serious doubts among the faculty about the English proficiency and likelihood of completion of the veterinary degree by foreign speaking students.

Enough Cash on Hand

Even if you are deemed fluent in the English language, you still have another big obstacle to overcome. U.S. immigration policy requires you to demonstrate that you have enough money in your bank to pay for four years of veterinary school tuition as well as room and board. It may cost as much as $80,000 per year to attend veterinary school and live either on- or off-campus. That means that, at least at schools that are this expensive, you will need to prove that you have $320,000 in savings and other liquid assets that you can use to pay for veterinary school. A home, for example, is not a liquid asset.

Many international students assume that there are grants and fellowships to help pay for a medical education, but this is not the case. Grants, assistantships, and fellowships are available in certain graduate programs, but they are almost never available in professional programs like veterinary medicine. Furthermore, any financial aid that is available is almost always given to U.S. citizens. Still, if you are wealthy and speak fluent English, your chances of going to veterinary school in the U.S. are good.

International Transcripts

An important point that should be mentioned is that transcripts written in a foreign language must be sent to an international transcript evaluation company. Once your transcript is translated into English and evaluated, you may then send this translation/evaluation to VMCAS and/or the veterinary schools to which you are applying for admission. Below are the three most commonly used firms from which you may obtain transcript translations and evaluations. Veterinary schools may not accept translations from other translating services, so please limit yourself to one of the three following firms.

Josef Silny & Associates, Inc.
International Education Consultants
7101 SW 102 Avenue
Miami, FL 33173
Phone: (305) 273-1616
Fax: (305) 273-1338
E-mail: info@jsilny.com
www.jsilny.com

World Education Services, Inc.
Bowling Green Station
New York, NY 10274-5087
Phone: (212) 966-6311
Fax: (212) 739-6100
(800) 937-3895
E-mail: info@wes.org
www.wes.org

Office of International Education Services
American Association of Collegiate Registrars and Admissions Officers
One DuPont Circle, NW, Suite 520
Washington, DC 20036-1135
Phone: (202) 293-9161
Fax: (202) 822-3940
E-mail: oies@aacrao.org
www.ies.aacrao.org

Another important institution for international students is the Educational Testing Service (ETS) and its Test of English as a Foreign Language (TOEFL) and TOEFL iBT tests. Their contact information is listed below.

Test of English as a Foreign Language -TOEFL®
P.O. Box 6151
Princeton, NJ 08541-6151
(609) 771-7100
www.ets.org/toefl

About the TOEFL iBT Test

The TOEFL iBT® (internet-based) test evaluates how well you combine listening, reading, speaking, and writing skills in order to perform academic tasks. This test is given at test centers where the internet is available. The TOEFL Paper-Based Test (PBT) is given only at test centers where there is no internet connection available. Most students take the TOEFL-iBT.

As with all standardized tests, we recommend that you thoroughly prepare and take practice tests before sitting for an official exam. Preparation materials are available at: www.ets.org/toefl/ibt/prepare.

Chapter Seven

The Importance of Large Animal Experience

W hen veterinary students finish their four years of veterinary school, they then prepare for a licensing exam—the North American Veterinary Licensing Exam (NAVLE®). The NAVLE assesses your knowledge of all species of animals, including large farm animals, food animals, wildlife, and exotic animals. Many students wish to practice veterinary medicine on small animals (also called companion animals) and may want little to do with large animals. The veterinary licenses issued by each state, however, allows one to practice veterinary medicine on all species, and thus the licensing exam must test your knowledge on all species, including large animals, food animals, and herd animal medicine (also referred to as population medicine). This is important to keep in mind as you gain the experience that you need to apply for admission.

Your Safety Is Their Concern

Large animals could injure you more seriously than most small animals. The admissions committees at veterinary schools ask important questions like: 'Does this student whom we are about to admit know how to keep herself or himself safe in the large animal facilities?' 'Does he or she know how to read an animal's behavior and know when to get out of a pen?' If these faculty members have any doubts about your ability to do this, they would simply move on to the next applicant who possesses experience with large animals. Again, you must learn about large animals and understanding basic safety is a concern of many faculty.

It should also be noted that the veterinary profession was not established to care for small animals. It was established centuries ago to provide for the medical needs of farm animals. State and provincial governments fund their veterinary schools for this same reason as well as for the needs of public health (many diseases cross over from animals to the human population). The veterinary profession is rooted in medicine and agriculture and the agricultural industry's need for farm animal medicine. Small animal medicine is a very recent development in the long history of veterinary medicine.

In general, veterinary schools do not want to admit anyone who has no large animal experience when other, similarly qualified applicants possess that experience. They recognize the need to teach about all species, small and large, and they know that the NAVLE will test your knowledge of all species.

Keep in mind, however, that your animal and veterinary experiences should never interfere with your academic program. Your academic preparation always comes first. There will always be time to arrange animal or veterinary experience after you complete your college program, but there may be very little time to repeat a course in which you did poorly because of your many time commitments outside of your academic program. Again, the best predictor of future academic performance is past academic performance, so do not overload yourself during your undergraduate academic program.

> The licensing exam must test your knowledge on all species, including food and farm animals.

When you volunteer at a veterinary clinic, be sure that you have both permission and time to shadow a veterinarian. One important result of any volunteer experience is to receive a good letter of evaluation from a veterinarian—not an office manager or a veterinary technician. If you have too little time to spend with the veterinarian, the veterinarian would not be able to write a genuine and complimentary letter. Some clinics are in great need of free help yet they forget that most pre-veterinary students volunteer in order to spend time with the veterinarian. Be sure to arrange quality time shadowing the veterinarian whenever you arrange any kind of animal experience.

Working or volunteering at zoos can be fun yet problematic when it comes to receiving a good letter of evaluation. Most zoos do not allow volunteers to shadow their veterinarians. If the letter that you receive is not written by a veterinarian, faculty usually deem it to be of little value.

Access to Large Animals

Most students who grow up in urban or suburban areas have a difficult time finding worthwhile experience with large animals. Fortunately, large animal experience can be planned into one's college program and accomplished in a number of different ways. One option is to attend a college that has large animals on campus (most colleges with an animal science program have large animals) and to work or volunteer with these animals on the weekends or whenever time permits. Another option is to select a college in a rural area with farm animals nearby. Another option is to take one summer during your college years and live with 'Uncle Bob' or 'Aunt Terry' out in the country. Although your relatives may not have large animals of their own, there may be a large animal veterinarian nearby who is willing to let you volunteer.

One cannot be shy when trying to line up large animal experience. Walking into a veterinary facility with a resume in hand and saying to the veterinarian, "I am a pre-veterinary student wanting to gain some large animal experience," is something that nearly all pre-veterinary students must do. Veterinarians are very familiar with this type of request. Indeed, there is a good chance that they themselves made this request to a veterinarian when they were applying to veterinary school. Don't be shy—they know exactly what you are up against.

Some veterinarians may be hesitant to allow you to volunteer because of liability issues. If the topic of liability comes up, be sure to say that you are fully covered by health insurance in case of any injury and that you are willing to sign a liability/injury waiver. (The issue of general liability outside of injury to yourself is an issue that you cannot solve. If the veterinarian wants free help and wishes to aid the future of the profession, he or she should be willing to take on a certain amount of general liability.) When volunteering to work for free, you also need to remember to tell the veterinarian that, at the end of the experience, you will want a formal letter of evaluation for veterinary school.

This may seem like nonsense to someone who wants to work with small animals, but because you will have to learn about large animals, the faculty members at the schools to which you apply will want to know that you know how to be safe around large animals.

Your Quantity of Hours is Important

It is important to obtain a solid number of hours working or volunteering before you ask for a letter of evaluation. Most letter of evaluation forms ask the evaluator how much time he or she has worked with the candidate. If the veterinarian says that he or she has only interacted with the candidate for a few hours, that letter does not have much weight with an admissions committee. We recommend that pre-veterinary students gain at least 200–300 hours of experience before asking a veterinarian to write a letter. Since you will want to have more than one letter, planning a timeline of experiences—within which each experience includes at least 200 hours—is valuable to do early on in your pre-veterinary years. Among the thousands of students who compete for spots in veterinary programs, many have strong profiles with good animal experiences, so you want to make sure to fully plan and gain valuable animal and veterinary experience before you begin to work on your applications.

If you have multiple opportunities from which to choose and you are unsure which to choose, you can contact your pre-veterinary advisor or PreVetAdvising.com.

We recommend
that pre-veterinary
students gain at
least 200–300
hours of experience
before asking a
veterinarian to
write a letter.

Chapter Eight

Animal Experience and Letters of Evaluation

As the last section explains, obtaining animal and veterinary experience is of little use in your effort to gain admission to veterinary school if you do not also obtain letters of evaluation. The terms "letter of evaluation" and "letter of recommendation" are used interchangeably by many, but because the largest part of any such letter is an evaluation and only its end is a recommendation, the term "letter of evaluation" is used throughout the book. The new knowledge that you gain in these experiences is very important, but documenting these experiences is also important. There are a number of variables in obtaining letters of evaluation of which you should be aware.

Be on the Same Page with Your Evaluators

Some veterinarians and professors who write letters of evaluation need reminders to write their letters. It is wise to kindly ask your evaluator to inform you when he or she has completed and sent your letter. If the evaluator does not inform you of this, then it may be appropriate to ask the evaluator if he or she has the time to send it. Again, some people who write letters need gentle reminders to finish the task.

Furthermore, be sure to tell your evaluator how many you are listing on your application for the experience about which the evaluator is writing. You may ask him or her if the number seems accurate; he or she may receive a phone call from the admissions office asking about this very thing. The last thing that you want is a major discrepancy between what you wrote on your application and what your evaluator wrote in the letter.

Don't Delay, Ask for the Letter Early

It is also important that you ask your evaluator for the letter as early as possible. If you mentioned your need for a letter of evaluation before you began your experience, do not assume that once the experience ends your evaluator will automatically begin writing a letter. To this end, it is important to set up your VMCAS application account in June of the year before you hope to enroll in veterinary school. By setting up the account early, you can identify your evaluators in the VMCAS system and notify them officially through VMCAS. If you are applying through VMCAS, your evaluator must submit his or her letter through the VMCAS system. Do not wait until August to set up your VMCAS account. If you wait, you will likely become frustrated when late September arrives and your letter is not yet completed. Most veterinary schools will want to see all of your evaluations before they begin to review your file.

If you ask your evaluators for their letters in August, or if you set up your VMCAS application account in August, be prepared to be frustrated and do not blame your evaluators for evaluations submitted at the very last minute. Keep in mind that your ordinary world of instant communication, of Facebook and other instantaneous online services, will slow down considerably when you apply for DVM admission. The application process is time-consuming, and you should begin it in June, not August.

The Ideal Combination of Letters

The ideal veterinary school admissions candidate would acquire at least two letters of evaluation from veterinarians, and each of these letters would be based on a minimum of 200–300 hours of experience with the evaluator. In a perfect world, one letter would come from a small animal veterinarian and one from a large animal veterinarian. A third letter is usually required from an advisor or academic mentor. Since many veterinary schools prefer to receive only three letters, any additional letters could be brought to your interview and offered to the interviewer. He or she may or may not accept these letters. Most applicants do not have more than two letters which document their animal and veterinary experience. Those who do have additional letters, however, may demonstrate a broader understanding of the profession and may be more likely to gain admission.

Most schools accept both a maximum and minimum of three letters. Table 4 can provide you with an idea of what may be required when you apply. It is important to check with each veterinary school about school-specific requirements in the year you apply to veterinary schools. The data which we have tracked year after year has changed yearly at least at one veterinary school.

The Nitty-Gritty on Letters

Most U.S. veterinary schools accept only the Electronic Letter of Recommendation (ELoR) that is provided by VMCAS. This reduces or eliminates the paper shuffle that admissions offices had previously managed for decades. It also speeds up the process of sending and receiving letters. When you begin your VMCAS application, you are asked to identify the three people who will write letters for you. You will enter their names and email addresses into the system and then VMCAS will inform them of your request by email and ask them to set up an account. When an evaluator submits an ELoR on your behalf, you will receive an email from VMCAS informing you that this letter has been received.

It has become necessary for veterinary schools to formally state that letters from family members or relatives are not acceptable in the admissions process. This is obviously a good policy. Furthermore, many veterinary schools will not accept letters that were several written years ago, or even recently written letters that are based on old experiences. Some schools provide only general guidelines for letters, while others specifically mandate who should write each letter. Required evaluators may include academic advisors, professors, research scientists, non-veterinary employment supervisors, or others.

While Table Four below is a good guide, requirements will likely be different by the time you apply. This chart is not meant to help you to avoid checking on each school's requirements. It is meant to give you a sense of what may be required of your application. As of 2015, if an applicant had letters from two veterinarians and one academic evaluation, she or he could meet the letter of evaluation requirements of a large majority of veterinary schools. However, just as prerequisite course requirements differ between veterinary schools, so do the requirements for letters of evaluation.

It is always advisable to begin by meeting the requirements of the veterinary school in your home state and to then determine which other schools' requirements are relatively easy to meet. In 2011, for example, one school required at least one letter be written by a licensed veterinarian. Since many animal science faculty members (who are, formally, veterinarians) are not required to keep active licenses, and some students obtain animal or veterinary experience on campus with these veterinarians, this requirement could pose a problem.

Many larger universities offer a "committee letter" or "composite letter" to all pre-health students. These letters are written by a committee of faculty members who know most students in their programs. These letters are acceptable for most health professions, but not, unfortunately, the veterinary profession. Veterinary schools are unique in that they prefer or, more commonly, require you to have shadowed a working veterinarian. Veterinary schools want to hear from the veterinarian, not from a committee. Only a small number of veterinary schools will accept a committee letter, so please try to avoid this type of letter and to obtain experience that a working veterinarian could evaluate. Committee letters may sometimes be substituted for a letter from an academic advisor, but even here veterinary schools usually prefer to hear from a single advisor.

If policies were set in stone and did not change from time to time, it would be easy to document these policies at the many veterinary schools. The reality, however, is that policies change and a chart of policies for one year may not be applicable the next. The following table is an attempt to summarize past policies in order to provide you with a general idea of what may be required of your application in the future.

The Personal Potential Index by the Educational Testing Service

The ETS Personal Potential Index (PPI) is a standardized information gathering tools used by some veterinary schools in addition or in place of the letter of evaluation. It provides reliable information on six personal attributes that graduate schools have indicated are critical for academic success. These areas include:

> Knowledge and creativity
> Communication skills
> Teamwork
> Resilience
> Planning and organization
> Ethics and integrity

If one of your veterinary schools requires the PPI, you would go to www.ets.org/ppi to set up a free account and request in their system that your evaluators complete a PPI. The PPI website then notifies your evaluators of your request. Your evaluators set up a free account and complete the twenty-four question survey about you.

If one evaluator completes many PPIs for many different applicants, the ETS system generates statistical information on how frequently your evaluator rates candidates high in each category. This helps the colleges understand whether the evaluator is typically a very generous evaluator or one who is very discerning in their evaluations. Since many evaluators tend to very generous to applicants and not very helpful to admissions committees, the PPI tool is one that helps admissions committees put things into perspective. This tool is relatively new and this author believes more colleges will be using it in the future.

To summarize the following chart of letter of evaluation requirements, two letters from veterinarians and one from an advisor would meet most veterinary schools requirements. This is our recommend combination of letters that we advise our clients to obtain. Since most international schools do not state their requirements for letters of evaluation, only American schools are listed below.

Table 4: Past Letter of Evaluation Requirements for U.S. CVMs

U.S. CVM at	Letter Type Required E=ELoR P=PPI	No. of Vets	Person Writing the Letter V= Veterinarian A= Advisor/Academic/Prof. S= Scientist/Science PhD e = Employer/Not a Vet
Auburn U.	3 E	1 Vet	1A, 1e or 1 additional Vet
UC, Davis	3 P	1-2	+ any combination
Colorado State U.	3 P	1	1e, 1A suggested
Cornell U., NY	3+ E	1	1A, 1V for each experience
U. of Florida	3 E	2	1A suggested
U. of Georgia	3 E	1	+ any combination
U. of Illinois	3-5 E	1	1A + any combination
Iowa State U.	3-6 E	1	+ any combination
Kansas State U.	3 E	1	1A
Louisiana State U.	3 E	1-2	(no additional information)
Lincoln Memorial U.	3 E	1	1A, 1e
Michigan State U.	3 E	1	No committee letter
Midwestern U.	3-6 E	1	+ any combination
U. of Minnesota	3 E	1	1A, no employer letter
Mississippi State U.	3 E	1	+ any combination
U. of Missouri	3-4 E	1	+ any combination
North Carolina S.U.	3 E	2	1 V or S
The Ohio State U.	3 E	2	(no additional information)
Oklahoma State U.	3 E	1	+ any combination
Oregon State U.	3 E	1	+ any combination
U. of Pennsylvania	3 E	1	1S or Science Professor
Purdue U.	3 E	1	+ any combination
U. of Tennessee	3 E	1	1A
Texas A. & M. U.	3 TX		use TX forms, any comb.
Tufts U.	3 E	1	1V or S, 1A, 1 Science Prof.
Tuskegee U.	3 E	1	2S
Virginia-Maryland Reg.	3 E	1	+ any combination
Washington State U.	3 E	1	1A
Western U. of Health Sci.	3 E		Any combination
Wisconsin U.	3 E	1 Vet	+ any combination

[1] Many CVMs do not want composite letters or those written by a committee.
Sources: AAVMC.org & CVM websites.

Chapter Nine

Activities Not Related to Veterinary Medicine

There are many activities from which to choose as you attend college. None of these activities should interfere with your academic program. Among the endless list of activities from which to choose are club activities, athletic activities, social activities (particularly on weekends), and student government. There are also many off-campus community service activities, and these are too numerous to list. Ideally, you would be involved in most of these activities, but realistically, you do not want to overload your schedule and over-commit.

So which activities are best? The correct answer to this question could only come from you. Engage yourself in activities that interest you the most. However, if this means partying on the weekends at the expense of everything else, straighten up and remember that you will be participating in a highly competitive admission process. Two measures of a good activity – for admissions purposes – are whether it can be documented through your student activities office and whether it will generate a letter of evaluation or document of participation.

It is also important to undertake a leadership experience. Many, if not all, veterinary schools want to see leadership experience of some kind on your application, even if it is simply serving as the captain of your intramural volleyball team. Leadership experience, which could range from serving as the president of a club to organizing and leading a band or chorus to starting a charitable effort and seeing it through, is almost a requirement of admission to veterinary school. You do not need to have extensive leadership experience, but having some leadership experience would help your application. Many colleges and universities hope that their graduates will become leaders who will shape the world and their professions. While most veterinarians may not become leaders of their profession, most veterinary schools want to believe their graduates will do just this.

It is also important to gain some community service or humanitarian endeavor. Admissions committees like to see an individual who has demonstrated some empathy toward the less fortunate, the ill, or the disabled. As a veterinarian, you will need to show empathy toward less fortunate clients who may need to put down their animals. It is not absolutely necessary to have community service, but it sure does help your application.

Whatever your extracurricular activities, you may also want to briefly discuss them in your application essay. You want to be able to say that you can handle a tough academic program but that you also have a life outside of your academic study.

We have a few important points on extracurricular activities.

Suggestions & Advice about Extracurricular Activities

1. Be very conservative during your first term at college. Do not take on any roles from which it is not easy to step down. Be a spectator who is able to leave an event early in order to do necessary homework.
2. If you are doing well academically, slowly become involved in more extracurricular activities. Adopt the philosophy that academic performance is of the utmost importance. Fun activities are secondary to your college experience.
3. Athletic activities are always a healthy choice, and most admissions committees like to see athletic achievement.
4. If you run for a club office (e.g., treasurer, president), be sure that you have the time for your office. Once you are elected, you cannot easily step down if you start to have academic problems.
5. If you do run into academic problems, seek help and, if necessary, back out of any commitments that you feel are stealing time away from your academic work.
6. Pay your club dues and have your activities recorded in the student activities office. Admissions staffs do check on the claims that are made on your application.
7. Gain some community or charitable experience to demonstrate your empathy for others.
8. Provide proof to the admissions committees that you can carry a full academic load and have a life outside of your studies. The veterinary schools want evidence that you will enjoy your DVM education.

Most importantly, have fun in college and grow to your full potential!

You will have many choices in college, and it is important that you make good choices that both enhance you personally and better your applications to veterinary schools.

Some students have unwanted documentation of public intoxication or, worse, drug use. Admissions offices do not want to see these records in your background. In fact, if you become involved with drugs and acquire a felony conviction, your future does not lie in medicine. Most felons cannot receive medical licenses. You should have fun in college, but if you are aiming for a medical education, it should be clean fun.

You should also keep your Facebook postings clean. Yes, admissions offices check Facebook postings of those students on their short list. If others have posted something undesirable about you, ask them to remove it or untag it yourself. The social media in which you participate becomes a public record. You will want to remember that admissions offices will check every possible record they can find to help themselves make decisions about applicants.

Be very conservative during your first term at college. Do not take on any roles from which it is not easy to step down. Be a spectator who is able to leave an event early in order to do necessary homework.

Chapter Ten

Ten Big Mistakes to Avoid

There are many mistakes that applicants make from which it is difficult to recover. Here is a list of the ten biggest mistakes that you must avoid:

1. Criminal conviction
2. Lying in your application
3. Prematurely overloading yourself
4. Terrible grades
5. Limited animal experience
6. Weak letters of evaluation
7. Claiming dual residency
8. Meeting only the minimum requirements
9. Unaccounted gaps of time
10. Not addressing a mistake or weakness

These mistakes could close the door to your full evaluation or obtaining an admissions interview. All of these mistakes are avoidable, but you must make good choices to avoid them. Below, we will discuss each of these mistakes.

1.   Criminal Conviction

A drug charge of any kind, any felony, or a sexual predator conviction could keep you out of veterinary school. In veterinary school, you will have access to a pharmacy. If you have a minor drug conviction, some committees may feel that you are too big a risk, especially given all of the other fine applicants. With a minor drug conviction, you should still apply, but be sure to address the conviction in your essay or explanation section. You might be able to say that you learned an important lesson that is of relevance to your future work.

A felony is much harder to own up to, and most felons are not able to obtain a medical license of any kind. Veterinary schools are understandably reluctant to admit anyone who cannot be licensed.

A sexual predator conviction may raise a student safety question: Why should a veterinary school admit someone who might harass or harm a fellow student?

Some states require their state-funded medical and veterinary schools to perform a criminal background check before each applicant's admission. If you have a criminal record, it will most likely come to light, whether you acknowledge this record or not. You do not want an admissions committee to discover something that you did not mention in your application. They would immediately wonder what else you might be hiding. So own up to any mistakes before the admission committee discovers them and make sure to tell the committee what you learned from your mistake.

2. Lying in Your Application

It is safe to say that all admission committees have been lied to. Since false statements and boastful claims are given to admission committees on a regular basis, admission officers are keen to verify as much information as they can. There are a number of ways that admission offices check and double-check the information that applicants provide. Offices routinely make telephone calls to student activities offices in order to check on the number and types of clubs and athletic teams in which an applicant claims membership. Calls to evaluators who write letters regarding the applicants' experiences are also routine. Criminal background checks are becoming more frequent and are now required in some states. Every applicant should be extremely careful not to exaggerate an accomplishment that they may not be given a chance to explain. An exaggeration can sometimes close the door to admission. Any deceit in an application could ruin your chances—even if you have high grades, great test scores, and broad animal experience.

3. Prematurely Overloading Yourself

As was discussed in previous chapters, many students make the mistake of taking on too many courses or other responsibilities before they know what they can actually handle. This does not only have an impact on your grades, it could have an impact on your overall wellbeing. Take it easy during your freshman year. It is important to *eventually* have a heavy load, given that veterinary study is significantly harder than undergraduate study. Just be sure to slowly increase your course load and to know your limits.

4. Terrible Grades

You may have a respectable GPA, but if you have one or two Ws, Ds, or Fs among an otherwise fine transcript, questions will be raised about whether you can survive a more rigorous academic program. If you apply with any of the above grades, briefly explain these grades in your essay or in the VMCAS explanation section. If you do not explain these grades, you may hurt your chance of admission.

Do not give an overly complicated explanation or one that is full of excuses. Get to the point quickly and clearly and then move on. Admissions committees like to see maturity in their applicants.

5. Limited Animal Experience

Limited animal and veterinary experience could make an otherwise excellent application look weak and undesirable. Do not waste your money applying early with very little animal or veterinary experience to show to the admissions committee. Be certain that you have at least one substantial experience—with 200 to 300 hours of experience—before applying. Ideally, you also want to have both large animal and small animal experience. Remember, experiences which have been evaluated after the application deadline are usually not considered.

6. Weak Letters of Evaluation

A letter of evaluation from a veterinarian who barely knows you and has an awkward time writing for you could hurt more than it helps. Applicants should have at least one letter from a veterinarian that is based on at least 200 hours of experience. Likewise, it is desirable to have two or three letters from veterinarians and that derive from both large animal and small animal experiences. Letters from previous wildlife or laboratory animal research experience are a real advantage, but are not necessary.

7. Claiming Dual Residency

When an applicant applies to veterinary schools through the Veterinary Medical College Application Service (VMCAS), he or she can claim residency in only one state. However, there are a small number of veterinary schools that do not participate in VMCAS. With these schools, it is possible—but unethical—to claim residency in another state to which the veterinary school gives priority. It is not unheard of for one admissions director to pick up the phone to call another director to ask whether a particular applicant was consistent in each application about his or her state residency. It is sometimes discovered that an applicant has claimed residency in two different states (which is almost always impossible and often illegal). In such a case, that applicant will likely be denied admission to both veterinary schools on the basis of this questionable behavior. Claiming dual residency is simply a dumb thing to do. We will discuss residency issues more fully in the next chapter.

8.   Meeting Only the Minimum Requirements

Admission committees set minimum requirements and these requirements are just that—the minimum requirements necessary for admission. With very rich applicant pools and thousands of applicants being rejected nationwide, why would admissions committees accept someone who has only accomplished the minimum? Doing only the minimum required for admission without complimenting these basics with additional coursework in the advanced biological sciences may make you less competitive. It is the rare student who has exceptional grades and test scores and can be admitted with minimal preparation. By adhering to only the minimum standards, most other students damage their chances of admission.

One common mistake that applicants make in this regard is not beginning their basic requirements during their freshman years. Since most courses in the advanced biological sciences require basic coursework, it is a big mistake not to begin General Biology and Inorganic Chemistry during your first year. (If you did not take Chemistry or Calculus in high school, speak with your pre-veterinary advisor about whether you should take an introductory course before taking General or Inorganic Chemistry.

9.   Unaccounted Gaps of Time

Occasionally, an applicant may have a summer or a year of time for which no activities or remarks are recorded in his or her application portfolio. This may mean that the applicant was working in a job that was unrelated to the profession and did not feel that it was necessary to mention it. What a big mistake!

On multiple occasions and at multiple professional schools, this author witnessed an admissions committee member say, "Maybe this gal was in prison?" or "Maybe he did absolutely nothing that summer." When committee members make remarks like these and there is no evidence to show the applicant was indeed busy with an unrelated endeavor, the committee may quickly move on to the next applicant.

Never leave a gap of time unaccounted for in your application. Make it obvious to the readers of your application that you have always been busy, even if these activities were not related to the veterinary profession.

10.   Not Addressing a Mistake or Weakness

We all have weaknesses, and some of us have failures the mention of which cannot be avoided in an application. If you have an obvious weakness or failure (perhaps an F in a college course, a court conviction, or a college suspension for poor behavior), be sure to address this weakness or failure somewhere in your application. As stated earlier, VMCAS offers an explanation section, and it is recommended that you use this section to explaining any weaknesses or mistakes. Keep in mind that you want to keep your essay as clean as possible of anything negative. Briefly explain your weakness or failure and then move on. Do not dwell on something that is negative; state only what you feel is minimally necessary to explain the situation. Saying nothing, however, is not an option. Avoiding anything that is negative would only create doubt and suspicion and you do not want such doubts attached to your applications.

Every
applicant should
be extremely
careful not to
exaggerate an
accomplishment.

Chapter Eleven

State Residency Affects Admission Decisions

Virtually all veterinary schools receive funding from their home state or province, and a condition to receiving this public money is that the veterinary schools must save a majority of their seats for home state (or provincial) residents. It is almost always easier to gain admission in the veterinary school in your home state than it is to gain admission elsewhere as an at-large or non-resident applicant. Some students change their state of residency, and in the end, they qualify as in-state residents in only one state and as at-large or out-of-state residents at all other veterinary schools.

There are a few private schools with modest or no state funding, and these schools tend to reserve fewer seats for in-state residents as compared to those schools with more generous state funding. They typically collect more tuition from non-residents, to make up the difference (in modest or no state funding).

U.S. Private Veterinary Schools with Fewer In-State Seats
Lincoln Memorial University
Midwestern University
Pennsylvania University
Tuskegee University
Tufts University
Western University of the Health Sciences

Cornell University, a private university, is somewhat unique because four of its twelve colleges are funded mostly by the State of New York, including the veterinary school. Cornell is the land-grant university of New York, but it remains a private institution. Due to state funding, Cornell's veterinary school has more in-state seats than out-of-state seats, even though it is privately run.

There are many states and provinces that do not possess or fund a veterinary school. Many of these states have entered into individual contracts with neighboring veterinary schools. These contracts require the veterinary school to save a defined number of seats for the residents of the contracting state. A listing of contractual arrangements can be found in the *Veterinary Medical School Admission Requirements* (VMSAR).

Fifteen Western states have formed the Western Interstate Commission for Higher Education (WICHE.edu). This commission was created in order to facilitate resource sharing among the higher education systems of the West. Veterinary schools in these states give preference to students from those WICHE states that do not have veterinary schools. Again, your chances of gaining admission increase whenever you apply to your home state veterinary school or to those veterinary schools that have individual or mutual contracts with your home state.

The WICHE states include Alaska, Arizona, California, Colorado, Hawaii, Idaho, Montana, Nevada, New Mexico, North Dakota, Oregon, South Dakota, Utah, Washington, and Wyoming. Note: Alaska does not participate in WICHE for veterinary medicine.

If you cannot afford to apply to every WICHE school, the first two schools that you ought to consider are Colorado State University and Washington State University. Their past ratios of applicants per seat are better than the ratios of the other schools.

Outside of WICHE, there are a few states that possess neither a veterinary school nor a contractual arrangement with a neighboring veterinary school. Students from these states and district (Alaska, the District of Columbia, Maine, New Hampshire, New Jersey, Rhode Island, and Vermont) are advised to move to a state with a veterinary school after checking with that school about residency qualification requirements. Furthermore, all applicants are advised to apply as in-state residents or as contractual residents at one veterinary school.

Table 6: Veterinary Schools with Contract Seats
This list does not include WICHE contracts.

CVM at:	State/Provincial Contracts
Auburn University	Alabama, Kentucky
Georgia, University of	Delaware, South Carolina
Iowa State University	Connecticut, Nebraska*, North & South Dakota
Kansas State University	North Dakota
Louisiana State Univ.	Arkansas
Minnesota, Univ. of	North Dakota (South Dakota reciprocity)
Mississippi State Univ.	South Carolina, West Virginia
Oklahoma State Univ.	Arkansas, Delaware
Tuskegee University	Kentucky, South Carolina
Virginia-Maryland Reg.	Virginia, Maryland, West Virginia
Washington State Univ.	Idaho, North Dakota
Prince Edward Is., U. of	New Brunswick, Newfoundland, Nova Scotia
Saskatchewan University	Alberta, British Columbia, Manitoba and Territories of Yukon, Nunavut, Northwest

*Nebraska has an educational alliance with Iowa's CVM.
Sources: CVM websites and AAVMC.org

Some states make it very easy to gain residency status for admissions purposes. In these states, it may take only six months or a year of residence to obtain residency (including Ohio, Missouri, and New York). Other states have very stringent rules about length of residency and other criteria before their veterinary schools will recognize official residency status. If you are thinking of moving to a state or province with a veterinary school in order to apply as an in-state resident, you are strongly advised to contact the state's veterinary school in order to understand all of the applicable residency qualification requirements.

With state budgets becoming smaller, in part due to a lingering Great Recession, residency requirements may become even stricter. It is very difficult to gather information about state residency requirements and list these requirements in a table because every state has different requirements. Likewise, different schools in anyone state may implement the requirements differently. In general, do not assume that residing in a state or province would automatically give you residency status. It is often necessary to file a state income tax return, change your voter registration, change your driver's license, and make other necessary changes in order to be considered an official resident of a state.

Voter Registration and Taxes

Some students are unsure of their residency statuses. A common cause of confusion is a student with two parents, each of whom lives in a different state or province. There are a multitude of other situations that could blur the issue of residency.

If you are in a blurry situation, there are two questions that can help to clarify your situation. The first question is, where are you registered to vote? You can only vote in one state or province, so voter registration is usually a good guideline of residency status.

The second question is, where do you pay state or provincial income taxes? Or, in what state are you claimed as a dependent on a parent's federal income tax? Taxes and voter registration provide clarity in most residency issues.

If you are not registered to vote, you should register soon for two reasons. You should want to document your residency status, and you should want to be a good citizen.

If you are claimed as a dependent on a parent's income tax form in a state without a veterinary school or in a state that contracts with another state's veterinary school, you may want to speak with your parent(s) about becoming independent for the purposes of improving your chances for DVM admission. Yes, your parent(s) may lose a big tax credit, but your chances of admission may increase dramatically if you can claim residency in a state that has a veterinary school. If you do become independent, plan this well before your application year. Many states have strict rules and timeframes surrounding the claim of independence and state residency.

Applicants who are in the U.S. military may occasionally possess dual state residency as recorded by the military. However, what the military states about your residency does not necessarily conform to what veterinary schools will perceive. If there is confusion about your residency, you could visit or contact the veterinary school or schools of your preference. Explain your situation and ask them how they would interpret your residency status.

Veterinary schools which receive state funding do not want to do anything which may jeopardize that funding. They will naturally be more conservative than you may wish. They must prepare for the eventual state audit which could question their internal residency determinations.

Do not assume that your state of residency recorded at your undergraduate college will automatically be accepted at the veterinary college. This author worked at three institutions in one state – New York State – at the City University of New York (Queens College), the State University of New York (Binghamton University) and at Cornell University. All three institutions in this one state had different residency rules. Perhaps this is a New York State phenomenon, but be prepared that your institutions could have similar byzantine rules about state residency.

Remember – always apply to your home state veterinary school or to a veterinary school with contractual commitments to your home state or province. Be sure to investigate state rules and complete any state residency forms and documentation which your veterinary school may require.

Always apply to your home state veterinary school, or to a veterinary school with a contractual commitment to your home state or province.

Chapter Twelve

Applying to Veterinary Schools

Applying to veterinary school is an almost full-time job. There are numerous forms to complete, both online and on paper. There are many deadlines to meet, essays to write, and—if you are successful—interviews to attend. The application year, which for currently enrolled undergraduates spans from May of your junior year to the following May, may be the busiest time of your undergraduate years.

A main focus of your early application endeavors should be to learn about the Veterinary Medical College Application Service (VMCAS). This service allows you to fill out one long application form and submit it to multiple veterinary schools. Almost all U.S. veterinary schools participate in VMCAS, and this common application allows you to check a box for each veterinary school to which you wish to apply. Texas A & M does not participate in VMCAS as its State has its own application service for medical and veterinary schools.

VMCAS will accept your personal statement, your letters of evaluation, and your transcripts and forward these to the veterinary schools which you selected. Once VMCAS has received all necessary materials from you, they will forward your application to the schools select. You must also complete supplemental applications by each school's deadlines. In the end, you will hear directly from your schools about your acceptance or rejection.

Once you decide how many schools to which you will apply, it is recommended that you create a file for each school. At the beginning of this file, you may want to keep a to-do list for that particular school, or you may prefer to have one master to-do list that includes all of the schools to which you have applied. Either way, the items on your list would include:

Register for the GRE
Write the personal statement/essay
Write short essay question answers for the supplemental applications
Complete the VMCAS application and submit it online by September 15
Complete each school's supplemental application
Complete transcript request forms for each school
Submit the supplemental applications by the posted deadlines
Pay the VMCAS fees, and supplemental application fees to your CVMs.
Respond to any correspondence from the veterinary schools or VMCAS
Prepare for interviews by learning what each CVM has to offer

You went through a similar process when you were a high school student. You probably had help from your mom or dad or perhaps a guidance counselor. Applying to veterinary schools, however, is much different than applying to college. First, you probably now live away from your parents and are on your own in this effort. Second, professional schools tend to have more requirements and hoops through which you must jump than do undergraduate admissions offices.

You may want to visit the VMCAS website sometime during your junior year in order to learn about the organization's latest policies and procedures. In fact, if you have time, it is recommended that you complete a sample application without submitting it one year before you plan to apply to veterinary school. This would take some stress off you during your busy and important senior year.

You would want to be sure to read about VMCAS policies and applicant expectations well before you begin the VMCAS application. They have official policies on these following topics:

Acceptance Deadline
Applicant Responsibilities
Applicant Data Privacy
Applicant SSNs
Evaluations, Materials Retention
Deadline Extension Policy
Evaluation Privacy Policy
Letters of Recommendation
Outstanding VMCAS Fee
Payments, Credit Cards
Student Transfers
Third Party Rankings
Applicant Data Retention
VMCAS Application Fee Policy
Materials to VMCAS Schools
VMCAS Processing Deadline

> A common and costly mistake many applicants make is not beginning the VMCAS application in June. August is very late to begin the application.

It is most important to know of applicant responsibilities. A helpful page to help you understand these is at: vmcas.helpgizmo.com/help/new-articles.

It should be noted that virtually all veterinary schools do not accept any materials such as applications, letters, transcripts, etc. after their posted deadline. It is important to have your evaluators and college registrars send their letters and transcript well before September 15. If, for example, if a transcript is sent yet not received at VMCAS, your application would be a waste of time and money.

VMCAS Is Expensive

VMCAS is very expensive if you want to apply to many veterinary schools. The typical applicant applies to about four or five schools.

VMCAS Application Fees for 2015-2016
1 CVM $195
2 CVMs $295
3 CVMs $395
Add $100 for each additional CVM
Source: AAVMC.org

It should be noted that all VMCAS participating colleges will see on your application the other VMCAS colleges to which you apply. If one were to apply to numerous VMCAS colleges, each college *may* get the impression that this applicant feels desperate and that impression *may* actually lessen your chances of gaining admission everywhere. When are too many applications to your disadvantage? Probably any number over ten may be too many. Again, the typical applicant applies to four or five veterinary schools.

In addition to the VMCAS fees, there are other fees such as:

1. CVM supplemental application fees
2. GRE or MCAT test registration fees
3. GRE or MCAT test score distribution fees
4. Transcript forwarding fees
5. Transportation costs to each interview

Unfortunately, there is little financial aid for applying to professional schools. You might need between $2,000 and $3,000 to apply to five or six colleges and then interview at three or four colleges. VMCAS does have a fee reimbursement program for those living below the poverty level, yet one would still need to pay the VMCAS fee upfront and then wait for it to be returned.

All American veterinary schools participate in VMCAS except Texas A. & M. Additional, many international schools participate including two Canadian schools, Guelph and Prince Edward Island; two Caribbean schools, Ross and St. George's; four European schools located in Dublin, Edinburgh, Glasgow, London; and in the Pacific region Massey University and the University of Sydney. Other schools belong to the AAVMC but do not mandate that your application come through VMCAS.

The Best Veterinary Schools

Pre-applicants and parents often ask us which veterinary school is the best. Our usual response is that there is no single best veterinary school. All students are different and all veterinary schools are different. Therefore, it would be impossible to say that one school is best for all students.

There is, however, a rule of thumb that could help you to begin to assess veterinary schools. First, you should know that veterinary schools are very expensive to operate. Without state government subsidies, they generally would lose money and would not be able to keep their doors open. Since veterinary schools are expensive to run, this author firmly believes that the best veterinary schools are in those states or provinces where there is a large tax base. The larger the tax base, the easier it is to properly fund a veterinary school. Generous government funding is essential to the running of any healthy and robust veterinary school. While veterinary schools in smaller states are generally very good, the best veterinary schools are usually found in states with a large tax base and large tax revenue.

There are, however, exceptions to most rules, and this one is no different. Colorado State University, for example, is located in a state with a moderate population and tax base. CSU, however, also receives significant funding through WICHE. Even though the state tax base may be smaller than that of many other states, CSU has one of the most highly regarded veterinary schools in the country.

You may be asking yourself: Doesn't the tuition that students pay keep the schools open? Tuition revenue in many veterinary schools makes up roughly 15 to 30% of the school's total revenue. Although it can be very expensive to attend veterinary school, these schools cannot always rely on tuition for the majority of their funding. They frequently rely on their states or provinces for a good portion of this funding. Veterinary students receive an expensive education and a good deal (i.e., a government subsidy) at the great majority of veterinary schools.

Another measure of a veterinary school is how many and what types of organized research centers exist at the school. If you have a keen interest in poultry medicine, for example, your veterinary school should have an organized research center on avian or poultry medicine. If your interest is in equine medicine, there should be an organized research center for equine medicine. The existence of numerous organized research centers at a veterinary school is an excellent sign of a fine veterinary school.

Dual Degree Programs

Many veterinary schools offer dual or combined degree programs such as a DVM/PhD program, DVM/MPH (Public Health) program, and a DVM/MBA program in addition to others. Likewise, a small number of veterinary schools have a scholarship program or Veterinary Scientist Training Program (VSTP)—sometimes funded by the NIH—that helps them to train future biomedical researchers. These programs usually provide free tuition for both the DVM and PhD programs, and may also include a stipend for your cost of living. If you are inclined to pursue a PhD in addition to the DVM, you would be wise to fully investigate these generous funding options.

The application process is a bit more involved. Usually, there are two applications required to be submitted directly to the veterinary schools. Don't wait to the last minute to investigate the extra application procedures if you are interested in these dual degree programs.

There is a coming shortage of veterinarians with PhDs. Many faculty members will be retiring soon and veterinary schools want to attract the best students into these dual programs to help fill future vacancies. If you do not have research experience, you would not have a chance of obtaining a free ride through both the DVM and PhD programs. If you like research and could see yourself working in academia or as a researcher, gain some credible laboratory research experience as an undergraduate student and think about applying to these dual programs. The profession needs more researchers and perhaps fewer practitioners.

Time and Money

It is important to budget both your time and money during the application year. Budgeting time can be difficult considering that you would likely be taking advanced biological science courses during this same period. It is recommended that you take the GRE by late June, which makes it possible for you to retake the exam in late August, if needed. It is also strongly recommended that you complete and submit the VMCAS application during the summer prior to your senior year. Once you finish the VMCAS application, you must begin your CVM supplemental applications. Most of these supplemental applications are due by September 15.

It is also important during the application year to apply for financial aid. You would have to do this before you know whether you have been accepted, wait-listed, or denied. There is more detail about this in Chapter Fifteen.

Chapter Thirteen

The Personal Statement
& Admissions Interview

The personal statement and the admissions interview are two mechanisms that allow admissions committees to get to know applicants. Both the personal statement and the admissions interview should be given significant preparation and attention. These two mechanisms will help you to distinguish yourself from the hundreds or even thousands of other applicants.

The following description of the personal statement is from the VMCAS application: "The personal statement should help the admission committee(s) learn something personal about the applicant, about his or her interest in veterinary medicine, and about your career goals." In brief, the admissions committees want to get to know the applicants which they are considering for admission. There are many possible topics which we will discuss soon.

Some applicants dread the personal statement. Those who do not have creative writing skills may be intimidated by the task of writing this essay. If you are struggling with your essay, you may want to follow this simple six-step process:

1. List potential topics to discuss (see below).
2. Write an outline incorporating one of the topics.
3. Write a rough draft of the essay.
4. Put it away for a few days and review it later.
5. Show it to a few people whom you trust for input.
6. Refine the essay again after receiving input.

There are many topics from which to choose when you write your personal essay. Here is a small list of popular topics from which many applicants select one or more as they begin to craft their statements:

1. Your motivation for becoming a veterinarian
2. Why you are well suited to be a veterinarian
3. The ideal characteristics of a veterinarian
4. Some event or experience that shaped who you are
5. What unique path you might pursue as a veterinarian
6. Club activities in which you have participated or may do so in the future

7. The nature or direction(s) of the profession
8. An animal-related experience that influenced you
9. Any significant experience that influenced you
10. Your family and socio-economic background
11. Something challenging that you overcame
12. The state of the world and the profession's role in that world
13. Something wrong with the profession and what you may do about it
14. Something humorous that relates to you or your application
15. Research that you have done—impress them with your knowledge!
16. Research you hope to do as well as what you already know about this research
17. Animal welfare issues & how the profession could help
18. A weakness or a mistake that you have overcome
19. Leadership experience that has shaped you

This list could be even longer. There is no wrong topic as long as your statement is positive and helps your reader get to know you. It is always a good idea to insert a little bit of humor if you have the gift of humor. Faculty members often become bored reading essay after essay. A small amount of humor could make your reader feel a bit more positive about you and your statement.

Sometimes, we must discuss something negative in the essay (e.g., bad grades or a youthful indiscretion of consequence). Never dwell too long on any negative topic. Be concise and quickly make your point. Then move on to something positive. If it is appropriate to do so, use the VMCAS explanation section and not the personal statement to explain these situations. As always, be concise.

In many cases, there is a word limit imposed on application essay questions. Do not exceed this word limit. Again, faculty often become bored reading application essays, and they may become grumpy if you grossly ignore the word limit. Likewise, be sure that your spelling and grammar are correct. Faculty members must score your essay and a sure way to lose points is by making them read something with poor spelling or grammar.

If you have difficulty writing your personal statement, it is recommended that you visit your pre-veterinary advisor for a book or purchase a book about how to write a good essay. Most advisors and all online bookstores have books on this topic.

PreVetAdvising.com offers an essay service. We would never write your essay for you. We may suggest ideas once we know a little about your background. We may also suggest major themes you may wish to incorporate into your personal statement. Having read thousands of essays, we can quickly find the weaker aspects of an essay and make suggestions to improve it.

What Not to Write

A typical essay would begin like this: "When I was five my dog was hit by a car; we rushed her to the veterinarian and ever since I knew I wanted to be a veterinarian." BORING! We read hundreds of these essays each year.

Do not put your readers to sleep about your love or passion for animals. We all like animals. Try to convince the faculty that you would bring some unique quality to the profession. Don't write about your passions if doing so would not distinguish you from the other applicants. This may be your only chance to shine – don't write about a love of animals – too many others do this, unwittingly to their disadvantage.

The Admissions Interview

While the personal statement can be a daunting task for some, virtually everyone is intimidated by the admissions interview. For those who are very nervous about being interviewed by faculty members, you should know that there are a handful of veterinary schools that do not interview at all.

U.S. Veterinary Schools Which Do Not Interview (at)
Colorado State University
Cornell University
University of Georgia
University of Iowa
North Carolina State University
University of Wisconsin

Your interview does not have to be intimidating, especially if you prepare well. One aspect of the interview that is important and over which you have total control is your appearance. It is important to dress well and to look professional.

Here are some dos and don'ts on interviews:
1. Do not have any piercings other than earrings (women only).
2. Do not use wild hair dyes. Your hair should look normal this one day.
3. Do not dress in anything less than a professional looking suit or outfit.
4. Cover up any tattoos as much as possible.
5. You are applying to a profession, so look professional.

Again, your appearance is totally under your control. A conservative professional appearance may give you more confidence as you engage in a long day of interviews with a variety of faculty, students, and staff.

Here is a simple list of things that can help to prepare you:

1. Do some research on the veterinary school and formulate informed questions that you might ask your interviewer when he or she gives you an opportunity to do so.
2. Prepare your dress or suit well before the day of the interview.
3. If you are traveling a long distance to the interview, give yourself plenty of time to encounter a delay of some kind. Arrive early—perhaps the night before—so that you arrive at the interview feeling settled and with your thoughts collected.
4. Prepare yourself for obvious questions, like:
   a. What interests you in the profession? Why do you want to be a veterinarian?
   b. Why did you apply to our veterinary school?
   c. What type of work do you want to do as a veterinarian?
5. Prepare any questions that you have for the DVM students who will give you a tour and have lunch with you.
6. Be prepared for questions on current issues and emerging diseases. Read the pages on Public Health and Issues at AVMA.org.
   Formulate your opinions and thoughts about these current issues.

Be sure to have questions of your own prepared (even if you know the answers) because you will probably be asked if you have any questions by the faculty member who is interviewing you. The last thing you want is to seem detached or just going through the motions of the interview. Engage your interviewer. Be sure to thank your interviewer, even if you did not like the interview experience.

Your pre-veterinary advisor should have literature about how to prepare for an admissions interview. If he or she does not have this material, online bookstores have books on both the admissions interview and interviews in general. Larger brick and mortar bookstores usually have a section called "College Guides." In this section, you can find all kinds of books about interviews, the personal statement, and more.

> Be sure to have questions of your own prepared (even if you know the answers) because you will probably be asked if you have any questions...

Chapter Fourteen

Rejected—Should You Re-Apply?

It is very disappointing not to be admitted to veterinary school after many years of hard work. Rejections are sent to at least half of the applicant pool nationwide and up to two thirds of the applicant pool when there is significant increase in applicants. If you are rejected, try to look at this rejection as a temporary bump in the road. There is always next year.

However, not everyone should immediately re-apply. If you do not significantly improve your application the following year, re-applying may be a waste of time, money, and effort. Many students do re-apply to veterinary school; in fact, each year a good portion of the national applicant pool is composed of re-applicants. If you are uncertain about re-applying, speak with your pre-veterinary advisor about the enhancements you will be making to your application portfolio. Get a sense from your advisor if these enhancements are significant enough to warrant re-applying.

Improve Your GRE Scores

There are almost always two aspects of one's application that can be improved upon. These are your GRE test scores and the breadth of your animal and veterinary background. If you feel that you did not have adequate time to prepare for the GRE test, you should put yourself through a more thorough preparation routine and then retake the exam. Most students can at least marginally improve their test scores by doing this. The same advice holds true for the MCAT and all other standardized tests.

Another consideration is whether you should take a private (and usually costly) test preparation course. Private test preparation courses work well for many students. Some students, however, find no advantage in taking these courses. You would not know whether such a course is right for you unless you actually take it. Generally speaking, if you took a test preparation course for the SAT or ACT and that course helped you to achieve a better score, you would probably find it advantageous to take a GRE (or MCAT) test preparation course.

One company, the Princeton Review, sometimes offers a money-back guarantee if their course does not improve your score. Other companies offer similar contracts from time to time. It is recommended that pre-veterinary students do all of the self-preparation that they can before they spend big bucks on a course. If you prepare yourself thoroughly, it is less likely that a private course will dramatically improve your score. If you could get a money-back guarantee for a private course, be sure to max out your self-preparation first; you might just get your money back and have a better understanding of the test!

Enhance Your Animal and Veterinary Experience

Adding to their animal and veterinary experience is a common enhancement re-applicants make. It is often difficult to have robust experience at the time of your first application. There are four categories of experience that you should try to have when re-applying to veterinary school. These categories are:

1. Small (or companion) animal experience
2. Large (or farm) animal experience
3. Wildlife or exotic animal experience
4. Research/laboratory animal experience

If you are weak in any one of these four areas at the time of your first application, try to find a volunteer experience between the time of your rejection and the next application deadline.

If you already possess this breadth of experience, you may want to consider accruing more significant experience in one of these four categories. Breadth of experience is usually preferred over depth of experience, but some faculty reviewers prefer depth. Needless to say, having depth in one of the four categories above cannot hurt your application.

Science Research

If you do not already have some, you may wish to consider gaining science research experience in order to improve your application. This may mean working as a lab assistant on an existing project, or setting up an independent study course or research topic in which you direct yourself. Serving as a lab assistant is the most common type of research experience that applicants tend to have.

If science research does not interest you to the point where you feel that you would be miserable in the laboratory, then do not attempt to serve as a lab assistant. Most veterinarians are not going to work as laboratory scientists, and for this reason science research is most often not required by veterinary schools. Such research is simply a feather in your cap if it appears in your application. If you like to do research, however, by all means pursue it. It may open doors for you.

If you apply to a DVM/PhD program, you will definitely want to have basic science research or biomedical science research in your portfolio. If you are interested in research in veterinary medicine, search the internet for "DVM/PhD programs." (In human medicine, these are called MSTPs, or Medical Scientist Training Programs.) Two veterinary schools, at the University of California, Davis and the University of Georgia, have a VSTP. These programs, and other combined DVM/PhD programs often provide free tuition for six or seven years, plus a stipend to cover room and board.

There are numerous opportunities for research out there. Veterinary medical research is both exciting and far-reaching. Searching the internet may make you aware of programs and awaken a latent interest in biomedical research.

Additional Science Coursework

As you think about re-applying, you may also want to revisit the breadth of your science coursework. If you have a minimal science background or if you have weak grades in some of your science courses, you may wish to take on additional science coursework. It is rarely recommended that you repeat a course unless you earned a D in a required course. It is usually better to take higher-level science courses and do well in those than it is to repeat a course. Veterinary schools have a wide variety of requirements, so there is plenty of opportunity to take additional sciences courses that may open additional doors to veterinary school. Take those courses that interest you the most. The greater your interest in a course, the better the grade that you are likely to earn.

Graduate School

Some students feel the need to go onto graduate school in order to enhance their veterinary school applications. This is a very big and serious decision, and it should always be reviewed with a pre-veterinary advisor or faculty mentor. We would never recommend graduate school to our students unless that graduate program was part of a second career path. To go to graduate school simply to enhance your veterinary school application is both costly and time-consuming. However, if graduate school opens another career door through which you would want to walk if veterinary school does not pan out, then a graduate program may be a good plan.

If you were weak in the sciences in your undergraduate program, then taking a science program at the graduate level would be prudent. If you were strong in the sciences, however, it is probably unnecessary to enroll in another science program.

Offshore and International Veterinary Schools

One last important consideration to make when re-applying is the option of offshore, English-speaking veterinary schools. Offshore schools in the Caribbean (including Ross University, Saint George's University, and Saint Matthew's University) are fine schools. The veterinary students who attend these schools have to do their clinical rotations (the last year of DVM program) at an onshore veterinary school – because these offshore schools do not yet have significant animal hospitals on their main campus. The offshore schools prepare you in the basic medical sciences and then place you, usually in an American veterinary school, in order to facilitate your clinical rotations.

There are other ways of gaining licensure, but these alternative methods are tedious and time-consuming. The best offshore DVM students have no problem obtaining clinical rotations at onshore veterinary schools. Weaker DVM students, however, may experience delays or difficulties obtaining their clinical rotations, and without completing rotations, you cannot easily receive your degree or become licensed.

Offshore English-speaking veterinary schools do a fine job at educating future veterinarians. However, they tend to be expensive and located in impoverished areas. American students are very wealthy in relation to the local populations around these schools, at least from the perspective of the local islanders. If you apply to an offshore school, and we encourage many students to do so, you would want to visit the school and the area in which it is located and inquire about life on the island. Do not ask officials for this information; ask veterinary students who have been on the island for a year or two. The crime rates in these places are not terrible and if you stay on campus most of the time you would have little over which to worry.

When you are off campus, just use common sense in protecting yourself and your belongings. Always travel with a companion if you are concerned about your safety. Ask other students about this issue and how they adjust to it. After all, these islands may have lower crime rates than some of our larger American cities.

European and Pacific Veterinary Schools

There are many other English-speaking veterinary schools around the globe. If you attend one of these international schools, you would come to know another part of the world and another way of life and receive your veterinary education at the same time. Overseas English-speaking veterinary schools that are accredited by the AVMA (see Appendix One) are probably more expensive than American veterinary schools, but they are often a very good option.

Never attend a foreign-speaking school unless you are fully fluent in the language of instruction. A medical education presents numerous foreign terms, usually in Greek and Latin, and some say that a medical education is itself a foreign language learning experience. Learning a foreign language in another foreign language while attempting to complete a rigorous medical education is simply academic suicide.

Keep in mind that attending a non-accredited foreign school would likely require you to receive licensure through the Educational Commission for Foreign Veterinary Graduates (ECFVG at avma.org) licensing program. This is a longer and less desirable way for North American veterinary students to become licensed veterinarians. However, if you speak Spanish fluently, the Latin America veterinary schools are an option.

We recommend to some of our clients to skip applying to American schools and begin applying to offshore schools once they are ready. There are many fine students who have either weak grades or weak GRE scores. If you are weak in both GPA and GRE scores, your chances are better at these offshore schools. Your pre-health advisor should be able to help you with this decision.

Deciding whether to re-apply to local veterinary schools, attend a different graduate school, or attend an international veterinary school are all difficult decisions. Find someone knowledgeable about veterinary school who can help you to review your ideas.

Chapter Fifteen

After Acceptance

For those applicants who earn an acceptance to veterinary school, congratulations! But remember, your work is not yet over. When you receive your acceptance letter, you may think that the process of enrolling in veterinary school has come to a conclusion, but there is important business to take care of between the months of January and May.

The April 15 Decision Deadline

The first thing that you need to know is that you will be given until April 15 to decide whether or not to accept your offer (when applying to U.S. schools). You may have multiple offers, but you can reserve only one seat after April 15. April 15 is an important date. By that date, you must accept your offer of admission or your seat may be given to someone on the waiting list.

Most applicants want to know about the financial aid that they will receive before April 15. In order to have a financial aid package by that time, U.S. students would need to file the FAFSA (Free Application for Federal Student Aid) by late January or early February. If you fail to complete the FAFSA in a timely manner, you probably would not have a financial aid package by April 15, but you would still have to give your non-refundable deposit to the school that you've chosen. One unfortunate truth of veterinary school applications is that financial aid packages are sometimes given after April 15, even when students file their FAFSA forms early.

It is important not only to accept your offer of admission by April 15; you should also inform any other veterinary schools that have extended you an offer that you will not be accepting their offers. As soon as you tell a veterinary school that you are not accepting its offer, the admissions officer at that school will be giving your seat to another deserving applicant. There is more detail about the April 15 agreement, how it affects, wait-listed students, your financial aid and other factors in a newsletter this author established as an Independent Contractor for the AAVMC at aavmc.org/prevetadvisor2.

The Agony of Being on a Wait List

There is no doubt – being on a wait list produces anxiety. The sooner a person with a full offer releases a seat – by telling the school he or she is attending elsewhere, the sooner a person on the wait list would be tapped. Some wait-listed students receive two offers close together and must turn down one of them quickly when it is after April 15. There were a couple of years in my ten year tenure at Cornell when so many students with offers waited until the very last minute to inform us that they would not be accepting our offer that we had to scramble to find wait-listed students (usually non-residents) who were still waiting for an offer.

Assume that you will be on a wait list. Assume that you will have to wait until April 10th to receive an offer. Would you not want to tell those students who possess full offers that it is important not only to make timely decisions, but that it is also important to notify the schools which they will not attend? If you do receive a full offer early in the process, remind yourself of the anxiety that you could be experiencing if you were wait-listed. Make your decision as quickly as you are comfortable doing so and inform every veterinary school that has extended you an offer of your decision. Do not wait until April 15 if at all possible. Pressure the financial aid office to give you an offer by April 10 - if that is holding up your decision.

When this author worked as Director of DVM Admissions at Cornell, I experienced a few rather humorous situations. I would call a wait-listed student who (unbeknownst to us) had already placed a deposit with his or her home state veterinary school. Nevertheless, the applicant wanted the Cornell offer simply to frame and hang on his or her wall. We were told this directly by a number of students. We were both flattered and bewildered that applicants would make others wait simply to receive and frame a letter. For this reason, we started to ask our alternates who we called near to April 15 if they needed time to decide or if they knew their decision. We had applicants say to us, "Will you send me the letter even though I know I will not accept the offer?" So we started asking our alternates about this.

After realizing that a number of students had this desire, we were able to speed up the process of enrolling our wait-listed students. We would express mail the offer with an oral agreement that the student would quickly and formally reject it. If you want an offer simply to hang on your wall, be upfront with this – it will save time and would be greatly appreciated.

Time is of the essence. If you want an offer from a school at which you are wait-listed simply to frame it, please tell them that upfront. The school will be pleased with your honesty and forthrightness and they will also be pleased that they can quickly move on to the next wait-listed student.

Anatomy and Physiology

As mentioned earlier, if you did not take anatomy or physiology in your undergraduate program, it is advisable to study these subjects formally or informally before veterinary school begins. These two subjects will be your first subjects in veterinary school. Knowing some of the terminology and the major concepts in these subjects would ease the transition from a relatively easy undergraduate program to an intense medical education.

The Formal April 15 Acceptance Deadline Agreement

You should be aware that no U.S. veterinary school can require you to accept an offer of admission before April 15. If a veterinary school requires you to accept an offer before this date, this school is breaking an agreement that all veterinary schools in the U.S. have signed. This agreement also prohibits veterinary schools from requiring applicants to accept financial aid or any scholarship offer before April 15. If someone exerts pressure on you to accept before April 15, feel free to call the Association of American Veterinary Medical Colleges to report the incident. With your confidential permission, the AAVMC may contact that person or school in order to remind them of the April 15 agreement. PreVetAdvising.com also handles these situations free of charge for both non-clients and clients on a confidential basis.

Once you have placed your deposit and thus reserved your seat at a veterinary school, you will be able to take a deep breath and relax—the process is almost over. The only thing left to do is to arrange your housing.

Searching for Housing

Some veterinary schools keep a housing resource list that you can access while you seek fall housing. Be sure to ask for housing information if it is not automatically given to you. There are usually university or college town websites available to help you search for housing. Be sure to ask the admissions folks for this information, especially if your search will be done from a distance.

Most students will rent an apartment or home for four years while a handful will buy property. Renters would likely need to sign a twelve-month lease for each of the four years that they attend veterinary school. College town landlords do not often provide anything shorter than twelve-month leases because they do not want summer vacancies.

We always advise veterinary students to begin their housing search by May and have it concluded by July 15th. Having an apartment or living arrangement set up by August 1st is a comfortable and happy feeling; you would have time to set up your apartment before veterinary school begins. We strongly advise you to arrive at school at least one week prior to the first day of orientation in order to settle into your apartment and to get to know the area. Once orientation and classes begin, you would not have time to finish settling your apartment or to drive around town to find retail stores. During the first week of classes, you will need to spend your time studying more than you probably desire.

Personal Relationships

It is valuable to reflect on your personal relationships before you begin veterinary school. Veterinary school is very time consuming and personal sacrifices are often needed in order to succeed in your medical education. If you are involved in a personal relationship when you are admitted to veterinary school, take some time to discuss with your partner the heavy time commitments you are likely to have. Many veterinary students find themselves studying six or seven days a week with time for only one night out per week. You may find this hard to believe, but after two weeks of veterinary school you will realize how intense a medical education really is.

> Having an apartment or living arrangement set up by August 1st is a comfortable and happy feeling...

Without some discussion and preparation, some partners cannot understand why their veterinary student partner is spending less time with him or her after veterinary school has begun. It is difficult to convince family and friends, even other pre-vets, how time consuming a medical education truly is.

Some personal relationships become troubled once veterinary school begins. It is important for both the veterinary student and the partner to be prepared for the lifestyle changes that will be brought on by the intensity of a veterinary education. Lack of good communication and perhaps some compromises could lead to academic trouble. Spending time away from studying in order to heal a troubled relationship could put undue pressure on any medical student.

At some veterinary schools, the partners of veterinary students have formed informal social groups—something like support groups—to help both the partner and the DVM student. If such a group exists where you attend veterinary school, encourage your partner to become involved. You and your partner may become friends with couples who can relate to the pressures that you would inevitably feel during veterinary school. Also, many graduate schools at these campuses have similar groups that are not just for veterinary students but all graduate students, and these groups offer the same type of support.

Communication is essential. Do not assume that your life will remain unchanged once you enroll. There could be many changes – almost all of them positive yet some may be difficult. Be prepared for the challenges ahead.

Chapter Sixteen

Veterinary Career Information

The American Veterinary Medical Association (AVMA) maintains a website with veterinary career information (www.avma.org). There are other sites and networks to which many schools are also subscribed. We encourage you to begin at the AVMA website for more information about veterinary careers. In particular, we encourage you to look through the statistical information that they have posted. We are grateful to the AVMA for allowing us to reprint portions of their information here. Other good sources of information are named below.

Please be advised, looking at salary averages can be both encouraging and discouraging. Starting veterinary salaries are low compared to the amount of debt that many veterinary graduates must carry. The first few years of practice could be financially difficult. Salaries for experienced veterinarians are much better. Below is a rough outline of how much veterinarians earn.

Generally speaking, there is an abundance of small animal practitioners and a shortage of large animal practitioners. There is also a shortfall of those with board certified specializations and a coming shortfall of those with both DVM and PhD degrees. It is always safe to say that those with more education would be more likely to earn larger salaries – and the chart below confirms this. If you could tolerate more than eight years of college, seriously consider continuing on in specialization training or in a PhD program. There is also a strong need for veterinarians with a public health degree and a variety of other degrees. It is rare to find a veterinarian with a law degree, but those who possess both will have many opportunities in government, industry and academia.

Career Connections and Information in Veterinary Schools

One of the best way to start networking and learning about career opportunities while in veterinary school is to join the Student Chapter of American Veterinary Medicine Association –SCAVMA. SCAVMA and their associate clubs – clubs which are usually focused on species of animals – will expose you to information and issues you may not know of now. They will bring in speakers and help you to begin networking while you are a DVM student. You would most definitely want to join SCAVMA and the clubs of your interest while in veterinary school.

Considering Salary and Lifestyle

Let us briefly discuss MD salaries and compare them to the DVM salaries below. Human medical doctors have higher salaries because society places more value on human life and human medicine than it does on animal life and veterinary medicine. If you are only interested in earning the highest possible salary, you should probably consider attending a human medicine program and become an MD. Generally, it is simply more lucrative to practice human medicine than it is to practice veterinary medicine.

There are also lifestyle considerations that you may also want to consider as you begin the process of becoming a veterinarian. Veterinarians are on call 24/7, but, just like human medicine, there are emergency centers and veterinary practices share emergency responsibilities. As a veterinarian, you may be less likely than an MD to be called in the middle of the night, especially if you share emergency responsibilities with other veterinarians and/or other veterinary practices.

As a veterinarian, it may also be easier to take time off to raise a family. Some in the profession theorize that this is one reason why many more women study veterinary medicine than do men. A rough ratio of women to men in veterinary schools is four to one, or about 80% female enrollment.

Table 7: U.S. Veterinarian Median Salaries, 2009

Private Clinical Practice	Salary	Typical Degree
Food animal exclusive	$103,000[1]	DVM
Food animal predominant	$ 91,000	DVM
Mixed animal	$ 85,000	DVM
Companion animal predominant	$ 91,000	DVM
Companion animal exclusive	$ 97,000	DVM
Equine	$ 85,000	DVM
Median Private Practice	**$ 97,000**	**DVM** (or VMD)

Public & Corporate Employment	Salary	Includes DVM+
College or University	$103,000	PhD
Federal Government	$103,000	MPH or PhD
State or Local Government	$106,000	MPH or PhD
Uniformed Services	$ 85,000	(no additional)
Industry (mostly Pharmaceuticals)	$148,000	PhD
Median Public & Corporate	**$109,000**	

Mean Starting Salary 2011	$70,000	DVM only

[1] This figure may represent a market response to a shortage of food animal veterinarians.
Source: AVMA

Please keep in mind that there are many considerations when deciding on a professional career path. Salary is only one of these considerations.

The following information may be reassuring to know that career networks are abundant in this profession.

Veterinary Career Network (VCN)

As the Veterinary Career Network states on their website, the VCN is "an alliance of professional associations with a combined registered membership of over 80,000 veterinary professionals with reach to over 100,000 individuals related to the veterinary profession. The Veterinary Career Network was developed by the American Veterinary Medical Association (AVMA) in 2006." Their website is at: www.veterinarycareernetwork.com.

Veterinary Schools with Full VCN Career Centers

Cornell University - College of Veterinary Medicine
Mississippi State University - College of Veterinary Medicine
North Carolina State University - College of Veterinary Medicine
University of Florida - College of Veterinary Medicine
University of Georgia - College of Veterinary Medicine
University of Wisconsin - School of Veterinary Medicine
University of Minnesota - College of Veterinary Medicine
University of Missouri - Columbia College of Veterinary Medicine
University of Tennessee College of Veterinary Medicine
Texas A & M University - College of Veterinary Medicine
Western University of Health Sciences - College of Veterinary Medicine
Ohio State University - College of Veterinary Medicine

Veterinary Schools Linked into VCN

Auburn University - College of Veterinary Medicine
Colorado State U. - College of Veterinary Medicine & Biomedical Sciences
Guelph University - Ontario Veterinary College - (Canada)
Iowa State University - College of Veterinary Medicine
Kansas State University - College of Veterinary Medicine
Louisiana State University - College of Veterinary Medicine
Michigan State University - College of Veterinary Medicine
Oklahoma State University - College of Veterinary Medicine
Purdue University - School of Veterinary Medicine
Tuskegee University - College of Veterinary Medicine
University of California Davis - School of Veterinary Medicine
University of Illinois - College of Veterinary Medicine
University of Saskatchewan - College of Veterinary Medicine
Washington State University - College of Veterinary Medicine

Do Veterinarians Need to Specialize?

The topic of veterinary specialization can be confusing. A veterinary degree and license would allow you to practice medicine with all species of animals. Most veterinarians focus their practices on either small or large animals, but this focus is not the same as a specialization.

A specialization in veterinary medicine usually requires an internship and residency in one of the formally recognized specialized areas of medicine, and this internship and residency occur after your four-year DVM program. Specializations in the veterinary profession are not centered on particular species; they are centered on a particular area of medicine (e.g., surgery, radiology, reproduction). Specialists go through more education than typical veterinarians, and with this extra education, they also tend to earn more money.

You do not need to specialize. You can begin practicing veterinary medicine as soon as you have (your):

Doctor of Veterinary Medicine (DVM or VMD) degree
Passed the NAVLE (North American Veterinary Licensing Exam)
Passed an additional state exam (in some states)
Issued a state license certificate.

If you think that you may want to specialize, however, you may decide to do so in your fourth year of veterinary school, or potentially later when you feel you are ready to specialize. Most veterinarians do not specialize; most are general practitioners who refer rare and difficult cases to specialists.

Below is a list of the various AVMA-approved specialty boards. It is reprinted here with permission from the AVMA. There are additional specialty organizations not formally recognized by the AVMA. Further sub-specialty information within each of the following organizations can be found at each organization's website.

American Board of Veterinary Practitioners
www.abvp.com
American Board of Veterinary Toxicology
www.abvt.org
American College of Animal Welfare
www.acaw.org/
American College of Laboratory Animal Medicine
www.aclam.org
American College of Poultry Veterinarians
www.acpv.info/
American College of Theriogenologists
www.theriogenology.org/

American College of Veterinary Anesthesiologists & Analgesia
www.acva.org/
American College of Veterinary Behaviorists
www.dacvb.org/
American College of Veterinary Clinical Pharmacology
www.acvcp.org
American College of Veterinary Dermatology
www.acvd.org
American College of Veterinary Emergency & Critical Care
www.acvecc.org
American College of Veterinary Internal Medicine
www.acvim.org
American College of Veterinary Microbiologists
www.acvm.us
American College of Veterinary Nutrition
www.acvn.org
American College of Veterinary Ophthalmologists
www.acvo.org
American College of Veterinary Pathologists
www.acvp.org/
American College of Veterinary Preventive Medicine
www.acvpm.org
American College of Veterinary Radiology
www.acvr.org
American College of Veterinary Sports Medicine & Rehabilitation
http://vsmr.org.p11.hostingprod.com/home
American College of Veterinary Surgeons
www.acvs.org
American College of Zoological Medicine
www.aczm.org
American Veterinary Dental College
www.avdc.org

The above organizations are officially recognized by the AVMA American Board of Veterinary Specialties (ABVS) Policies and Procedures. Their website is at: avma.org/education/abvs/abvs_pp.asp.

The AVMA has outlined career opportunities and workforce needs. A portion of their work is reprinted below, with their permission and our gratitude.

Career Information

Today's veterinarians are in the unique position of being the only doctors trained to protect the health of both animals and people. They are not only educated to meet the health needs of every species of animal, but they play an important role in environmental protection, food safety, and public health.

Caring Professionals

According to consumer surveys, veterinarians consistently rank among the most respected professionals in the country. Currently more than 82,000 veterinarians actively practice in the United States and the profession is growing at a rate of approximately 3% per year.

In taking the **Veterinarian's Oath**, a new graduate solemnly swears to use his or her "scientific knowledge and skills for the benefit of society through the protection of animal health, the relief of animal suffering, the conservation of animal resources, the promotion of public health, and the advancement of medical knowledge."

Protecting the Health of Animals and Society

Employment opportunities for veterinarians are almost endless and include private or corporate clinical practice, teaching and research, regulatory medicine, public health, and military service.

Private or Corporate Clinical Practice

In the United States, approximately 67% of veterinarians are engaged in the exciting field of private or corporate clinical practice. Of these, many treat only pets such as dogs, cats, birds, small mammals (e.g., hamsters, guinea pigs), reptiles, and fish. Other veterinarians limit their practice to the care of farm/ranch animals and advise owners on the best approaches to production medicine; some exclusively treat horses; and still others treat a combination of all species.

Teaching and Research

Veterinarians may use their education to instruct veterinary students, other medical professionals, and scientists. Veterinary college/school faculty members conduct research, teach, and develop continuing education programs to help practicing veterinarians acquire new knowledge and skills.

Veterinarians employed in research at universities, colleges, governmental agencies, or in industry, are dedicated to finding new ways to prevent and treat animal and human health disorders. The public can credit veterinarians for many important contributions to human health. For example, veterinarians helped control malaria and yellow fever, solved the mystery of botulism, produced an anticoagulant used to treat some people with heart disease, identified the cause of West Nile virus infection, and defined and developed surgical techniques for humans, such as hip and knee joint replacements and limb and organ transplants helping animals before humans.

Veterinarians who work in pharmaceutical and biomedical research firms develop, test, and supervise the production of drugs and biological products, such as antibiotics and vaccines, for human and animal use. These veterinarians usually have specialized training in fields such as pharmacology, virology, bacteriology or pathology.

Veterinarians are also employed in management, technical sales and services, and other positions in agribusinesses, pet food companies, and pharmaceutical companies. They are in demand in the agricultural chemical industry, private testing laboratories, and the feed, livestock, and poultry industries.

Regulatory Medicine

Veterinarians who work for the U.S. Department of Agriculture's Food Safety and Inspection Service (FSIS) or in a state department of agriculture protect the public from unhealthy livestock and unsafe meat and poultry. They ensure food products are safe and wholesome through carefully monitored inspection programs.

To prevent the introduction of foreign diseases into the United States, veterinarians are employed by state and federal regulatory agencies to quarantine and inspect animals brought into the country. They supervise interstate shipments of animals, test for diseases, and manage campaigns to prevent and eradicate diseases such as tuberculosis, brucellosis, and rabies that pose threats to animal and human health.

United States Department of Agriculture (USDA) veterinarians in the Animal and Plant Health Inspection Service (APHIS) monitor the development and testing of new vaccines to ensure their safety and effectiveness. APHIS veterinarians are also responsible for enforcing laws for the humane treatment of animals. Other branches of the USDA such as the Agricultural Research Service (ARS) and the Cooperative State Research,

Education, and Extension Service (CSREES), also have employment opportunities for veterinarians.

Public Health

Veterinarians serve as epidemiologists in city, county, state, and federal agencies investigating animal and human disease outbreaks such as food-borne illnesses, influenza, rabies, Lyme disease, and West Nile viral encephalitis. They also help ensure the safety of food processing plants, restaurants, and water supplies.

Veterinarians working in environmental health programs study the effects of pesticides, industrial pollutants, and other contaminants on animals and people. At the U.S. Food and Drug Administration (FDA), Veterinarians evaluate the safety and efficacy of medicines and food additives. Veterinarians also work at the Agricultural Research Service, Fish and Wildlife Service, Environmental Protection Agency, Centers for Disease Control and Prevention, National Library of Medicine, and National Institutes of Health. Many of these veterinarians serve in the U.S. Public Health Service Commissioned Corps.

Veterinarians also help to protect the health and safety of animals and people in the Department of Homeland Security through their work in developing antiterrorism procedures and protocols.

Military Service

Veterinarians in the U.S. Army Veterinary Corps are at the forefront in protecting the United States against bioterrorism. They are responsible for food safety, veterinary care of government-owned animals, and biomedical research and development. Officers with special training in laboratory animal medicine, pathology, Microbiology, or related disciplines, conduct research in military and other governmental agencies.

In the U.S. Air Force, veterinarians serve in the Biomedical Science Corps as public health officers. They manage communicable disease control programs at air force bases around the world and work towards halting the spread of HIV, influenza, hepatitis, and other infectious diseases through education, surveillance, and vaccination.

Other Professional Activities

Zoologic medicine, aquatic animal medicine, aerospace medicine (shuttle astronauts), animal shelter medicine, sports medicine (race horses, greyhounds), animal-assisted activity and therapy programs, and wildlife management also employ veterinarians.

Is Veterinary Medicine Right for You?

Today's veterinarians are extremely dedicated and willing to work long, difficult hours to save the life of an animal or help solve a public health crisis. Among the personal attributes that contribute to a successful career in veterinary medicine are:

A scientific mind – Individuals who are interested in veterinary medicine should have an inquiring mind and keen powers of observation. Aptitude and interest in the biological sciences are important. Veterinarians must maintain a lifelong interest in scientific learning, and must genuinely like and understand animals.

Good communication skills – Veterinarians should be able to meet, talk, and work well with a variety of people. Compassion is an essential attribute for success, especially for veterinarians working with pet owners who form strong bonds with their pets.

Management experience – Many work environments (e.g., private or corporate clinical practice, governmental agencies, and public health programs) require that veterinarians manage other employees. Basic managerial and leadership skills training make these positions much more rewarding.

A Bright Future

Employment opportunities for veterinarians are expected to keep pace with those of other professions. Positions exist for which postgraduate education in Molecular Biology, laboratory animal medicine, toxicology, immunology, diagnostic pathology, environmental medicine, or other specialties is preferred or required. The benefit of using scientific methods to breed and raise livestock, poultry, and fish, together with a growing need for effective public health and disease control programs, will continue to demand the expertise of veterinarians.

Chapter Seventeen

About PreVetAdvising.com and Its Services

This educational consulting firm is dedicated to distributing information about how to gain admission to veterinary schools and to help individual students to improve their credentials for veterinary school admissions.

We are the only educational consulting firm that focuses exclusively on veterinary school admissions. We are also the only private educational admissions consulting firm that offers financial aid to disadvantaged students. As you will see, we offer many of our services free of charge.

Free Services for Students

We feel that it is important to help all students. As mentioned earlier, admissions consulting follows a seasonal schedule. During the off-season (October–May), we are willing and able to help students who possess few resources at no charge. We also do this to a lesser extent during the summer, but at that time there is usually a waiting list.

Many students access these free services and give themselves an advantage over others who do not. We encourage you to use our free services, and apply for financial aid for our other services. The sooner you contact us, the more affective we can be at improving your qualifications and applications.

PreVetAdvising.com offers at no charge:

- A 30-minute initial assessment over the phone (October-May). Interested students must use our short and quick to complete Free Consultation Form at our website.
- A 15-minute initial assessment (June–September). Please keep in mind that this service is offered only as time permits.
- Information on prerequisites, school policies, and deadlines, as well as illustrated tuition differences for non-residents at our website.
- A 30-minute high school student/parent consultation session (October–May).

Services for Students for a Fee

After completing our short Free Consultation Form and undergoing the corresponding phone appointment, you may decide that you wish to hire us one or more of the following:

1. Phone appointments for general advisement after our free consultation
2. Our review and suggested revisions of your applications
3. Our review and suggested revisions of your VMCAS essay
4. Our review and suggested revisions of your other essays
5. Admissions interview coaching, usually by phone
6. Long-term coaching with almost unlimited access to our services.

All of these services include short follow-up email conversations. Often people have additional questions which did not come out during the phone conversation. Additional services are listed at our website. Our rates as well as our financial aid information are posted at PreVetAdvising.com.

Our clients have had a 79% acceptance rate over many years into veterinary school. The U.S. national average acceptance rate has been about 48%. Students and parents often tell us that they wish they found this book and our services earlier as we could have helped them make important decisions. The sooner you contact us, the sooner we can help you.

Student Financial Aid for Our Services

Our rates for various services are always publicly posted to ensure fairness and openness about what we do and what we charge. To learn more about our services and our rates, visit PreVetAdvising.com/services.

Why do we offer financial aid when we are a private firm? We firmly believe that all students, whether wealthy, middle-class, or disadvantaged, should have equal access to our services. We use standard criteria, similar to the criteria used by colleges and universities, to assess our students' ability to afford our services. Guidelines regarding our financial aid are available at our website.

The APVMA

We encourage pre-veterinary clubs to join the American Pre-Veterinary Medical Association (APVMA). This national organization offers resources and information to all pre-veterinary clubs. Their national symposium is hosted at a different veterinary school campus every year, and it is usually held in March. Their website is at: APVMA.org.

Our Free Services for Pre-Veterinary Clubs

We are happy to speak to your club or any gathering of ten pre-veterinary students or more free of charge. Our PowerPoint presentation includes both basic information and advice about how to improve veterinary school applications.

Your school or pre-veterinary club only pays for travel-related expenses; there are no speaking fees. If your timing is flexible and Mr. Piekunka plans to be in your area on other business (he travels frequently), these travel costs may be shared with a neighboring college's pre-veterinary club. Please email Mr. Piekunka's assistant at assistant@PreVetAdvising.com for more information.

The Following Services Are Free to Clubs:
-Get Into Veterinary School-PowerPoint (travel *may* not be at our expense)
-Free advice on restructuring a pre-veterinary club charter
-Free listing in our Pre-Veterinary Club Directory
-Phone or Skype appointments to help establish a new pre-veterinary club

If your club would like free advertisement, please complete the club form at PreVetAdvising.com/index.php/forms. If you are trying to initiate a club, please complete the club initiation form that is available at our site. This form may help you to find other pre-veterinary students on your campus who also want to form a club but do not know of others students who are interested in veterinary medicine. One question we ask is whether your pre-veterinary club is interested in networking with other pre-veterinary clubs in your city or region. This is a way of sharing resources and putting smaller clubs into contact with larger clubs. If you respond affirmatively to this question, we will happily put you in touch with other pre-veterinary clubs.

If you are considering initiating or joining a pre-veterinary club, remember that it looks great on any application to veterinary school to list a title as an officer in a pre-veterinary club. It also looks great to list a club office if you apply to other professional schools and for general employment. This means that it is worthwhile to participate in your local pre-veterinary club even if you change your mind about your future profession. If your club has money to cover travel costs and a dwindling membership, try inviting a speaker like Mr. Piekunka or a local veterinarian to speak on your campus. Bringing in a speaker tends to inspire new membership, or at least new interest, in an organization or club. Another interest builder may be to visit a veterinary school as a club or group. If your college owns a van for such occasions, your club may be able to save some dollars. Let us know if we can help you to build membership or raise awareness of your club.

Free Services for Pre-Health Advisors

All pre-health advisors who seek information about veterinary school admissions are welcome to call or email Mr. Piekunka for one-on-one advice. He is happy to help the students of advisors through the advisor or by coming to speak with pre-veterinary students in a group setting.

Free Services for Undergraduate Institutions

PreVetAdvising.com maintains a list of undergraduate colleges and universities that offer solid pre-veterinary preparation. There are six criteria that an institution must meet to be listed. Briefly stated, to be included a pre-veterinary program must:

- Have an advisor who is a member of the National Association of Advisors for the Health Professions (NAAHP.org) or one of its regional associations;
- Have a vibrant pre-veterinary or pre-health club that is officially recognized by a student activities office or similar campus entity;
- Offer all of the basic science courses discussed in Chapter One on an annual basis;
- Offer Genetics, Microbiology, and Statistics as well as the courses listed on page 14 every other year if not annually;
- Be a selective four-year college and offer a four-year degree program in which all of the above-mentioned courses may apply toward that four-year degree;
- (Should) Maintain a list of veterinarians (and organizations) with whom pre-veterinary students may gain animal or veterinary experience.

A college or university cannot purchase a placement on our list. They either meet the criteria or they do not. Evaluation for inclusion is done by PreVetAdvising.com and we have sole discretion in determining which colleges are placed on the list. Canadian and international undergraduate institutions are welcome to apply for inclusion in our list of recommended colleges. The free application is found under Forms at our site, PreVetAdvising.com.

To see the listing of schools that meet this requirement please see Appendix Seven or visit PreVetAdvising.com. The list in Appendix Seven may change within months after this book is published. It is important to check the PreVetAdvising.com website as some schools may be taken off the updated list and others may be added.

If you are an advisor, admissions officer, or college administrator and wish that your school would be added to our list of colleges that offer pre-veterinary studies, please apply at our site. Our application is free and may be obtained by emailing Mr. Piekunka's assistant at: assistant@PreVetAdvising.com.

We also provide a list of agricultural schools and colleges where pre-veterinary students may gain animal experience. These lists are printed in the appendices of this book and at our website.

Privacy Policy at PreVetAdvising.com

PreVetAdvising.com website does not place cookies or any files on your computer. We may collect personal information from those students who request our billable services. We keep all potential and actual client information confidential secure; we do not sell, share, or otherwise release any information (unless required by law) to others. Your information is safe with us and any services we provide to you will be private and will always remain confidential.

If you email us, we will send one response email and perhaps one follow-up email, if necessary. You will not receive spam from us—we dislike spam as much as you do!

We do not collect full date of birth or other personal information, like your Social Security number (unless you apply for financial aid). Please do not send us your date of birth or Social Security number unless we specifically ask for these. If you send us an application for us to review, please delete your full date of birth and include only your year of birth. Delete any other unique individual identifiers you do not wish for us to see.

We hope you will give yourself the same advantage other students give themselves by contacting us for our free services.

Do You Have Comments About Our Book?

If you have comments, suggestions, or feedback that you would like to give the author of this book, please send us an email with your thoughts. This book is republished every few years and your thoughts and comments are important to us. Please consider emailing us at: assistant@PreVetAdvising.com.

A Message from the Author

Dear Pre-Veterinary Student:

I wish you the very best in preparing for the veterinary profession. I hope you found the chapters useful. About half of the upcoming appendices should be useful for high school students and the other half should be useful for college and returning adult students.

Remember, the best predictor of future academic performance is past academic performance.

Please contact me if you need advice or guidance while preparing for veterinary school.

Good luck!
Mr. Piekunka

Appendix One

Veterinary Schools & Umbrella Organizations

Alabama
Auburn University
College of Veterinary Medicine
104 Greene Hall
Auburn University, AL 36849
Telephone: 334-844-4546
vetmed.auburn.edu

Tuskegee University
School of Veterinary Medicine
Tuskegee, AL 36088
Telephone: 334-727-8174
tuskegee.edu

Arizona
Midwestern University
College of Veterinary Medicine
19555 North 59th Avenue
Glendale, AZ 85308
Telephone: (623) 572-3215
midwestern.edu/programs-and-admission/az-veterinary-medicine.html

California
University of California
School of Veterinary Medicine
Davis, CA 95616-8734
Telephone: 530-752-1360
vetmed.ucdavis.edu

Western University of the Health Sciences
College of Veterinary Medicine
309 E Second Street
Pomona, CA, 91766-1854
Telephone: 909-469-5628
westernu.edu/cvm.html

Colorado
Colorado State University
College of Veterinary Medicine and Biomedical Sciences
Fort Collins, CO 80523
Telephone: 970-491-7051
cvmbs.colostate.edu

Florida
University of Florida
College of Veterinary Medicine
PO Box 100125
Gainesville, FL 32610
Telephone: 352-392-4700
vetmed.ufl.edu

Georgia
University of Georgia
College of Veterinary Medicine
Athens, GA 30602
Telephone: 706-542-3461
vet.uga.edu

Illinois
University of Illinois
College of Veterinary Medicine
2001 South Lincoln Avenue
Urbana, IL 61802
Telephone: 217-333-2760
cvm.uiuc.edu

Indiana
Purdue University
School of Veterinary Medicine
1240 Lynn Hall
West Lafayette, IN 47907
Telephone: 765-494-7607
vet.purdue.edu

Veterinary Schools of the AAVMC, continued

Iowa
Iowa State University
College of Veterinary Medicine
Ames, IA 50011
Telephone: 515-294-1242
vetmed.iastate.edu

Kansas
Kansas State University
College of Veterinary Medicine
Manhattan, KS 66506
Telephone: 785-532-5660
vet.ksu.edu

Louisiana
Louisiana State University
School of Veterinary Medicine
Baton Rouge, LA 70803-8402
Telephone: 225-578-9900
vetmed.lsu.edu

Massachusetts
Tufts University
Cummings School of Veterinary Medicine
200 Westboro Road
North Grafton, MA 01536
Telephone: 508-839-5302
tufts.edu/vet

Michigan
Michigan State University
College of Veterinary Medicine
G-100 Veterinary Medical Center
East Lansing, MI 48824
Telephone: 517-355-6509
cvm.msu.edu

Veterinary Schools of the AAVMC, continued

Minnesota
The University of Minnesota
College of Veterinary Medicine
1365 Gortner Avenue
St. Paul, MN 55108
Telephone: 612-624-9227
cvm.umn.edu

Mississippi
Mississippi State University
College of Veterinary Medicine
Mississippi State, MS 39762
Telephone: 662-325-3432
cvm.msstate.edu

Missouri
University of Missouri-Columbia
College of Veterinary Medicine
Columbia, MO 65211
Telephone: 573-882-3877
cvm.missouri.edu

New York
Cornell University
College of Veterinary Medicine
Ithaca, NY 14853
Telephone: 607-253-3700
vet.cornell.edu

North Carolina
North Carolina State University
College of Veterinary Medicine
4700 Hillsborough Street
Raleigh, NC 27606
Telephone: 919-513-6210
cvm.ncsu.edu

Veterinary Schools of the AAVMC, continued

Ohio
The Ohio State University
College of Veterinary Medicine
1900 Coffey Road
Columbus, OH 43210
Telephone: 614-292-1171
vet.ohio-state.edu

Oklahoma
Oklahoma State University
College of Veterinary Medicine & Center for Veterinary Health Sciences
Stillwater, OK 74078
Telephone: 405-744-6595
cvm.okstate.edu

Oregon
Oregon State University
College of Veterinary Medicine
Corvallis, OR 97331
Telephone: 541-737-2098
vet.orst.edu

Pennsylvania
University of Pennsylvania
School of Veterinary Medicine
3800 Spruce Street
Philadelphia, PA 19104
Telephone: 215-898-5438
vet.upenn.edu

Tennessee
University of Tennessee
College of Veterinary Medicine
2407 River Drive
Knoxville, TN 37996
Telephone: 865-974-7262
vet.utk.edu

Veterinary Schools of the AAVMC, continued

Lincoln Memorial University
College of Veterinary Medicine
6965 Cumberland Gap Parkway
Harrogate, TN 37752
Telephone: (800) 869-9000, ext. 6676
lmunet.edu/cvm/admissions/index.shtml

Texas
Texas A&M University
College of Veterinary Medicine & Biomedical Sciences
College Station, TX 77843
Telephone: 979-845-5051
cvm.tamu.edu

Virginia - Maryland
Virginia Polytechnic Institute
Virginia-Maryland Regional College of Veterinary Medicine
Blacksburg, VA 24061
Telephone: 540-231-7666
vetmed.vt.edu

Washington
Washington State University
College of Veterinary Medicine
Pullman, WA 99164
Telephone: 509-335-9515
vetmed.wsu.edu

Wisconsin
University of Wisconsin-Madison
School of Veterinary Medicine
2015 Linden Drive West
Madison, WI 53706
Telephone: 608-263-6716
vetmed.wisc.edu

Veterinary Schools of the AAVMC, continued

Canada

Alberta
University of Calgary
Faculty of Veterinary Medicine
Calgary, Alberta T2N 4N1
Telephone: 403-210-3961
vet.ucalgary.ca

Ontario
University of Guelph
Ontario Veterinary College
Guelph, ON N1G 2W1
Telephone: 519-824-4120
ovcnet.uoguelph.ca

Prince Edward Island
University of Prince Edward Island
Atlantic Veterinary College
550 University Avenue
Charlottetown, PE C1A 4P3
Telephone: 902-566-0882
upei.ca/~avc

Quebec
Université de Montréal
Faculté de Médecine Vétérinaire, C.P. 5000
Saint Hyacinthe, PQ, J2S 7C6
Telephone: 450-773-8521
medvet.umontreal.ca

Saskatchewan
University of Saskatchewan
Western College of Veterinary Medicine
52 Campus Drive
Saskatoon, SK, S7N 5B4
Telephone: 306-966-7447
usask.ca/wcvm

Veterinary Schools of the AAVMC, continued

Central America

Costa Rica
Universidad VERITAS
Escuela de Medicina y Cirugía Veterinaria
San Francisco de Asís
San Rafael de Coronado
Telephone: (506) 2292-7639
E-mail: info@veterinariaveritas.ac.cr

Mexico
Universidad Nacional Autonoma de México
Facultad de Medicina Veterinaria y Zootecnia
Ciudad Universitaria, Mexico
Telephone: 52 (55) 5622 5855
fmvz.unam.mx

Caribbean Schools
These schools are commonly referred to as Off-Shore schools

Ross University
School of Veterinary Medicine
Basseterre, Saint Kitts
Telephone: 869-465-1080
rossu.edu/veterinary-school/

St. George's University
School of Veterinary Medicine
Grenada, West Indies
Telephone: 800-899-6337
sgu.edu/school-of-veterinary-medicine/index.html

St. Matthew's University
School of Veterinary Medicine
Grand Cayman, KY1-1209
Cayman Islands
Telephone: 345-745-3199
stmatthews.edu/school-of-veterinary-medicine.shtml

Veterinary Schools of the AAVMC, continued

Europe

Denmark
University of Copenhagen
Faculty of Life Sciences
Bülowsvej 17, Frederiksberg, DK-1870, Denmark
Telephone: +45 35 33 20 47
life.ku.dk/english.aspx

Ireland
University College Dublin
School of Agriculture, Food Science & Veterinary Medicine
Belfield, Dublin 4, Ireland
Telephone: 353 1 716 6100
ucd.ie/agfoodvet

The Netherlands
State University of Utrecht
Faculty of Veterinary Medicine
3508 TD Utrecht, The Netherlands
Telephone: 31 30 253-4851
vet.uu.nl

United Kingdom
University of London
The Royal Veterinary College
London NW1 OUT, England, UK
Telephone: 44 (0)20 7468-5000
rvc.ac.uk

University of Glasgow
Faculty of Veterinary Medicine
Glasgow, G61 1QH, Scotland, UK
Phone: 44 (0)141 330-5700
gla.ac.uk/faculties/vet

The University of Edinburgh
Royal School of Veterinary Studies
Edinburgh EH9 1QH, Scotland, UK
Telephone: 44 131 650-1000
vet.ed.ac.uk

Veterinary Schools of the AAVMC, continued

Pacific

Australia
Murdoch University
Division of Veterinary and Biomedical Sciences
Murdoch, WA, Australia
Telephone: 61 8 9360 2566
vet.murdoch.edu.au

The University of Melbourne
Faculty of Veterinary Science
Werribee, VIC, Australia
Telephone: 61 3 9731 2261
vet.unimelb.edu.au

University of Queensland
School of Veterinary Science
Gatton, 4343, Australia
Telephone: 61 7 5460 1834
uq.edu.au/vetschool/

The University of Sydney
Faculty of Veterinary Science
NSW 2006, Australia
Telephone: 61 2 9351 6936
vetsci.usyd.edu.au

Japan
University of Tokyo
Graduate School of Agricultural and Life Sciences
1-1-1, Yayoi, Bunkyo-ku, Tokyo, Japan, 11-8657
u-tokyo.ac.jp/en

Philippines
Central Luzon State University
Science City of Munoz
31020 Philippines
Telephone: +63 44 4565877
clsucvsm.edu.ph

Veterinary Schools of the AAVMC, continued

New Zealand
Massey University
College of Sciences, Institute of Veterinary, Animal, and Biomedical Sciences
Palmerston North
New Zealand
Telephone: 64 6 350-5714
ivabs.massey.ac.nz

South Korea
Seoul National University
1Gwanak-gu, Seoul
South Korea
En.snu.ac.kr/apply/info

North American Veterinary Umbrella Organizations

American Veterinary Medical Association
1931 North Meacham Road, Suite 100
Schaumburg, IL 60173
Telephone: 847-925-8070
avma.org

Association of American Veterinary Medical Colleges
1101 Vermont Avenue, NW, Suite 301
Washington, DC 20005
Telephone: 202-371-9195
aavmc.org

Veterinary Medical College Application Service (of the AAVMC)
Toll Free: 877-862-2740
aavmc.org

American Pre-Veterinary Medical Association
apvma.org (Led by students – no permanent address)

Appendix Two

Veterinary Technology Programs

The following programs are listed for those students who may not pursue admission to veterinary medical school yet want to explore the possibility of a veterinary technology education. Being a veterinary technician is a wonderful alternative for those who do not feel a doctoral program is the right fit. There is a shortage of veterinary technicians and your job security in this field should be solid for years to come.

In some cases when a Bachelor's degree is offered, veterinary technician students may be able to pursue both a veterinary technology degree and a pre-veterinary program. For the most current information on accredited veterinary technology programs, visit avma.org.

Please note: We indicate below which schools are on "Probationary Accreditation." This denotation means that the college has some problem to fix before they could regain full accreditation. Initial Accreditation simply means the program is new and will eventually be fully accredited

Canada

Ridgetown College, University of Guelph
Veterinary Technology Program
Main Street East
Ridgetown, Ontario N0P 2C0
519-674-1666

Puerto Rico

University of Puerto Rico
Veterinary Technology Program
Medical Sciences Campus
San Juan, PR 00936-5067
787-758-2525, ext. 1051 or 1052
Bachelor of Science

Alabama

Faulkner State Community College
Veterinary Technology Program
1900 Hwy 31 South
Bay Minette, AL 36507
251-580-2100

Jefferson State Community College
Veterinary Technology Distance Learning Program
2601 Carson Road
Birmingham, AL 35215-3098
205- 856-8519

**Veterinary Technology
Programs, continued**

Arizona

Mesa Community College
Veterinary Technology/Animal
Health Program
1833 W Southern Avenue
Mesa, AZ 85202
480-461-7488
Associate of Applied Science

Penn Foster College
Veterinary Technician Distance
Education Program
14300 N Northsight Blvd, Suite
120
Scottsdale, AZ 85260
800-275-4410
Associate in Science

Pima Community College
Veterinary Technology Program
8181 E Irvington Road
Tucson, AZ 85709-4000
520-206-7414
Associate of Applied Science

Pima Medical Institute-East
Valley
Veterinary Technology Program
2160 S Power Road
Mesa, AZ   480-898-9898
Associate of Applied Science
Initial Accreditation

Pima Medical Institute-Tucson
Veterinary Technology Program
3350 E Grant Road
Tucson, AZ 85716
520-326-1600
Associate of Applied Science
Initial Accreditation

Arkansas

Arkansas State University-Beebe
1000 Iowa Street
PO Box 1000
Beebe, AR 72012
501-882-4572
Associate of Applied Science

Heritage College-Little Rock
Veterinary Technology Program
1309 Old Forge Drive
Little Rock, AR   501-708-0909
Associate of Occupational Studies
Initial Accreditation

**Veterinary Technology
Programs, continued**

California

California State Polytechnic
University-Pomona
Animal Health Technology Prg.
3801 W Temple Ave
Pomona, CA   909-869-2136
Bachelor in Animal Health
Science

Carrington College-Citrus Heights
7301 Greenback Lane, Suite A
Citrus Heights, CA 95621
916-722-8200
Associate of Science

Carrington College-Pleasant Hill
Veterinary Technician Program
380 Civic Drive, #300
Pleasant Hill, CA 94523
925-609-6650
Associate in Science

Carrington College-Pomona
901 Corporate Center Drive
Pomona, CA 91768
916-388-2884
Associate of Science

Carrington College-Sacramento
Veterinary Technology Program
8909 Folsom Blvd
Sacramento, CA 95826
916-361-1660
Associate in Science

Carrington College-San Jose
Veterinary Technician Education
Program
6201 San Ignacio Ave
San Jose, CA 95119
408-360-0840
Associate in Science

Carrington College-San Leandro
Veterinary Technology Program
170 Bayfair Mall
San Leandro, CA 94578
510- 276-3888
Associate in Science

Carrington College-Stockton
Veterinary Technician Education
Program
1313 West Robinhood Drive
Stockton, CA 95207
209-956-1240 x 44116
Associate in Science

Cosumnes River College
Veterinary Technology Program
8401 Center Pkwy
Sacramento, CA   916-691-7355
Associate in Science

Foothill College
Veterinary Technology Program
12345 El Monte Road
Los Altos Hills, CA 650-949-7203
Associate in Science

**Veterinary Technology
Programs, continued**

Los Angeles Pierce College
Veterinary Technology Program
6201 Winnetka Ave
Woodland Hills, CA 91371
818-347-0551
Associate in Science

Mount San Antonio College
Animal Health Technology
Program
1100 N Grand Ave
Walnut, CA 91789
909-594-5611
Associate of Applied Science

Pima Medical Institute-Chula
Vista
780 Bay Blvd, Suite 101
Chula Vista, CA 91910
619-425-3200
Associate of Applied Science
Initial Accreditation

Platt College-Alhambra
Veterinary Technology Program
1000 S Fremont Ave, Suite A9W
Alhambra, CA 91764
626-300-5444
Associate of Science
Initial Accreditation

Platt College-Ontario
Veterinary Technology Program
3700 Inland Empire Blvd
Ontario, CA 91764
909-941-9410
Associate of Science
Initial Accreditation

Platt College-Riverside
Veterinary Technology Program
6465 Sycamore Canyon Blvd
Riverside, CA 92507
951-572-4300
Associate of Science
Initial Accreditation

San Joaquin Valley College
Veterinary Technology Program
295 East Sierra Ave
Fresno, CA 93710
866-544-7898
Associate of Science
Initial Accreditation

Yuba College
Veterinary Technology Program
2088 N Beale Road
Marysville, CA 95901
530-741-6962
Associate in Science

Veterinary Technology Programs, continued

Colorado

Bel-Rea Institute of Animal Technology
1681 S Dayton Street
Denver, CO 80231
800-950-8001
Associate of Applied Science

Colorado Academy of Veterinary Technology
2768 Janitell Road
Colorado Springs, CO 80906
719-432-6384
Associate of Applied Science
Initial Accreditation

Colorado Mountain College
Veterinary Technology Program
Spring Valley Campus
3000 County Road 114
Glenwood Springs, CO 81601
970-945-8691
Associate of Applied Science

Community College of Denver
Veterinary Technology Program
1070 Alton Way, Bldg 849
Denver, CO 80230
303-365-8300
Associate of Applied Science

Front Range Community College
Veterinary Research Technology Program
4616 S Shields
Ft Collins, CO 80526
970-226-2500
Associate of Applied Science

Pima Medical Institute-Colorado Springs
3770 North Citadel Drive
Colorado Springs, CO 80910
719-482-7462
Associate of Applied Science

Pima Medical Institute-South Denver
Veterinary Technology Program
13750 E Mississippi Ave
Aurora, CO 80012
800-477-PIMA (7462)
Associate of Applied Science
Initial Accreditation

Connecticut

Middlesex Community College
Veterinary Technology Program
100 Training Hill Road
Middletown, CT 06457
860-343-5800
Associate of Science
Initial Accreditation

**Veterinary Technology
Programs, continued**

NW Connecticut Community
College
Veterinary Technology Program
Park Place East
Winsted, CT 06098
860-738-6490
Associate in Science

Delaware

Delaware Technical and
Community College
Veterinary Technology Program
PO Box 610, Route 18
Georgetown, DE 19947
302-855-5918
Associate of Applied Science

Florida

Eastern Florida State College
Veterinary Technology Program
1519 Clearlake Road
Cocoa, FL   321-433-7594
Associate in Science

Florida A&M University
Veterinary Technology Program
4259 Bainbridge Highway
Quincy, FL   850-599-3000
Bachelor of Science
Initial Accreditation

Heritage Institute-Fort Myers
Veterinary Technology Program
6630 Orion Drive, Suite 202
Fort Myers, FL   239-936-5822
Assoc. of Occupational Studies
Initial Accreditation

Hillsborough Community Coll.
Veterinary Technology Program
Plant City, FL   813-757-2157
Associate in Science

Institute of Technical Arts
Veterinary Technology Program
493 Semoran Blvd
Casselberry, FL   321-280-5482
Associate of Science
Initial Accreditation

Miami-Dade College
Veterinary Technology Program
950 NW 20th Street
Miami, FL   305-237-4473
Associate in Science

Pensacola State College
Veterinary Technology Program
1000 College Blvd
Pensacola, FL   850-484-1000
Associate of Science
Initial Accreditation

Veterinary Technology Programs, continued

Sanford Brown College-Fort Lauderdale
Veterinary Technology Program
1201 West Cypress Road
Fort Lauderdale, FL
954 -308-7400
Associate in Science
Initial Accreditation

Sanford Brown College-Jacksonville
Veterinary Technology Program
10255 Fortune Parkway
Jacksonville, FL
904-380-3757
Associate of Specialized
Technology-Initial Accreditation

Sanford Brown College-Tampa
Veterinary Technology Program
3725 W Grace Street
Tampa, FL 33607
877-809-2444
Associate in Science
Initial Accreditation

St Petersburg College
Veterinary Technology Program
St Petersburg, FL 33733
727-341-3652
Associate in Science
Distance Learning Program
Associate in Science
Bachelor of Applied Science

Georgia

Athens Technical College
Veterinary Technology Program
800 US Highway 29N
Athens, GA   706-355-5107
Associate of Applied Science

Fort Valley State University
Veterinary Technology Program
1005 State University Drive
Fort Valley, GA   478-825-6353
Bachelor of Science

Gwinnett Technical College
Veterinary Technology Program
5150 Sugarloaf Pkwy
Lawrenceville, GA 30043
770-962-7580
Associate of Applied Science

Ogeechee Technical College
Veterinary Technology Program
1 Joe Kennedy Blvd
Statesboro, GA 30458
912-688-6037
Associate of Applied Science

Southwest Georgia Technical C.
Veterinary Technology Program
15689 US Highway 19 North
Thomasville, GA 229-225-4096
Associate in Applied Science
Initial Accreditation

**Veterinary Technology
Programs, continued**

Hawaii

Windward Community College
Veterinary Technology Program
45-720 Keaahala Road
Kaneohe, HI   808-235-7400
Associate in Science
Initial Accreditation

Idaho

Broadview University-Boise
Veterinary Technology Program
2750 E Gala Ct
Meridian, ID 83642
208-577-2900
Associate in Applied Science
Initial Accreditation

Brown Mackie College-Boise
9050 W Overland Rd, Suite 100
Boise, ID 83709
208-321-8828
Associate of Applied Science
Initial Accreditation

College of Southern Idaho
Veterinary Technology Program
315 Falls Ave
Twin Falls, ID 83303-1238
208-733-9554 ext. 2408
Associate of Applied Science

Illinois

Joliet Junior College
Agriculture Sciences Depart.
1215 Houbolt Road
Joliet, IL   815-280-2746
Associate of Applied Science

Parkland College
Veterinary Technology Program
2400 W Bradley Ave
Champaign, IL 61821
217-351-2224
Associate of Applied Science

Rockford Career College
1130 S Alpine Road, Suite 100
Rockford, IL 61108
815-965-8616
Associate of Applied Science

Veterinary Technology
Programs, continued

Southern Illinois Collegiate
Common Market (SICCM)
Includes schools at:
John A Logan College at
Carterville;
Kaskaskia College at Centralia;
Rend Lake College at Ina;
Shawnee Community College at
University of Illinois;
Southeastern Illinois College at
Harrisburg;
Southern Illinois University at
Carbondale;
Southern Illinois University at
Edwardsville.
3213 South Park Avenue
Herrin, IL 62948
618-942-6902
Associate of Applied Science

Vet. Tech Institute, Fox College
18020 Oak Park Ave
Tinley Park, IL 60477
708-636-7700
Associate of Applied Science

Indiana

Brown Mackie Coll.Fort Wayne
Veterinary Technology Program
3000 E Coliseum Blvd
Fort Wayne, IN   260-484-4400
Associate of Applied Science
Initial Accreditation

Brown Mackie Coll.South Bend
Veterinary Technology Program
3454 Douglas Road
South Bend, IN   574-237-0774
Associate of Science

Harrison College - Indianapolis
Veterinary Technology Program
6300 Technology Center Drive
Indianapolis, IN   317-873-6500
Associate of Applied Science

Harrison College-Evansville
Veterinary Technology Program
4601 Theater Drive, Evansville,
IN 47715   812-476-6000
Associate of Applied Science

Purdue University
School of Veterinary Medicine
Veterinary Technology Program
West Lafayette, IN 47907
765-496-6579
Associate of Science
Bachelor of Science
Distance Learning Program -
Associate of Science

The Vet Tech Institute at
International Business College at
Fort Wayne
5699 Coventry Lane
Fort Wayne, IN 46804
260-459-4500
Occupational Associate

Veterinary Technology Programs, continued

The Vet Tech Institute at
International Business College -
Indianapolis
7205 Shadeland Station
Indianapolis, IN 46804
317-813-2300
Occupational Associate

Iowa

Des Moines Area Community
College
Veterinary Technology Program
2006 S Ankeny Blvd FFA_EC
Ankeny, IA   800-362-2127
Associate of Applied Science

Iowa Lakes Community College
Veterinary Technology Program
19 South 7th Street
Estherville, IA 51334
712-262-7141
Associate in Applied Science
Initial Accreditation

Iowa Western Community College
Veterinary Technology Program
2700 College Road, Box 4-C
Council Bluffs, IA 51502
712-325- 3431
Associate of Applied Science

Kirkwood Community College
Animal Health Technology
Program
6301 Kirkwood Blvd, SW
Cedar Rapids, IA 52406
319-398-4978
Associate of Applied Science

Muscatine Community College
Veterinary Technology Program
152 Colorado Street
Muscatine, IA 52761
563-288-6001
Initial Accreditation
Associate in Applied Science

Northeast Iowa Community
College
Veterinary Technology Program
1625 Hwy 150 South
Calmar, IA 52132
800-728-2256
Initial Accreditation
Associate of Applied Science

Kansas

Brown Mackie College-Kansas
City
Veterinary Technology Program
9705 Lenexa Drive
Lenexa, KS 66215
913-749-5038
Associate of Applied Science
Initial Accreditation

Veterinary Technology Programs, continued

Kentucky

Brown Mackie College-Salina
Veterinary Technology Program
2106 South 9th Street
Salina, KS 67401
785-309-2150
Associate of Applied Science
Initial Accreditation

Colby Community College
Veterinary Technology Program
1255 S Range
Colby, KS 67701
785-460-5466
Associate of Applied Science

Colby Community College
Veterinary Technology Distance
Education Program
1255 S Range Ave
Colby, KS   785-462-3984
Associate of Applied Science
Initial Accreditation

Independence Community College
1057 W College
Independence, KS   620-332-5433
Initial Accreditation
Associate of Applied Science

Wright Career College
Veterinary Technology Program
10720 Metcalf Ave
Overland Park, KS
800-555-4003
Initial Accreditation
Associate of Applied Science

Brown Mackie College -
Louisville
3605 Fern Valley Road
Louisville, KY   502-968-7191
Associate of Science
Probationary Accreditation

Morehead State University
Veterinary Technology Program
25 MSU Farm Drive
Morehead, KY   606-783-2326
Bachelor of Science
Associate of Applied Science

Murray State University
Animal Health Technology
Program
100 AHT Center
Murray, KY   270-762-7001
Bachelor in Science

Owensboro Community and
Technical College
Veterinary Technology Program
1501 Frederica Street
Owensboro, KY   270-686-4400
Associate in Applied Science
Initial Accreditation

Veterinary Technology Programs, continued

Louisiana

Baton Rouge Community College
Veterinary Technology Program
201 Community College Drive
Baton Rouge, LA 225-216-8000
Associate of Applied Science
Initial Accreditation

Delgado Community College
5200 Blair Drive
Metairie, LA 70001
504-671-6234
Associate of Applied Science

Northshore Technical College
Veterinary Technology Program
Greensburg, LA 70441
225-222-4251
Associate of Applied Science
Initial Accreditation

Northwestern State University of Louisiana
Veterinary Technology Program
225 Bienvenu Hall
Natchitoches, LA 71497
318-357-5323
Associate Degree
Bachelor of Science

Maine

University of Maine Bangor Campus
Veterinary Technology Program
85 Texas Avenue, 217 Belfast Hall, Bangor, ME
207-262- 7852
Associate of Science
Probationary Accreditation

Maryland

Essex Campus of the Community College
Of Baltimore County
Veterinary Technology Program
7201 Rossville Blvd
Baltimore, MD 21237
410-682-6000
Associate of Applied Science

Massachusetts

Becker College
Veterinary Technology Program
964 Main Street
Leicester, MA 01524
508-791-9241
Associate in Science
Bachelor of Science

Holyoke Community College
Veterinary Technician Program
303 Homestead Ave
Holyoke, MA 01040-1099
413-538-7000
Associate in Science

Veterinary Technology Programs, continued

Mount Ida College
Veterinary Technology Program
777 Dedham Street
Newton, MA   617-928-4545
Associate in Arts
Bachelor of Animal Science

North Shore Community College
Veterinary Technology Program
1 Ferncroft Road
Danvers, MA 01923
978-762-4000
Associate of Applied Science

Michigan

Baker College of Cadillac
Veterinary Technology Program
9600 East 13th Street
Cadillac, MI 49601
231-775-8458
Associate of Applied Science

Baker College of Clinton
34950 Little Mack Ave
Clinton Township, MI 48035
586-790-9430
Associate of Applied Science

Baker College of Flint
Veterinary Technology Program
1050 W Bristol Rd, Flint, MI
800-964-4299 or 810-766-4153
Associate of Applied Science

Baker College of Jackson
Veterinary Technology Program
2800 Springport Road
Jackson, MI 49202
517-789-6123
Associate of Applied Science

Baker College of Muskegon
Veterinary Technology Program
1903 Marquette Avenue
Muskegon, MI 49442
800-937-0337 or 231-777-5275
Associate of Applied Science

Macomb Community College
Veterinary Technician Program
44575 Garfield Road
Clinton Township, MI 48044
586-286-2096
Associate of Applied Science

Michigan State University
College of Veterinary Medicine
Veterinary Technology Program
East Lansing, MI 48824
517-353- 7267
Certificate, Bachelor of Science

Wayne County Community
College District
Veterinary Technology Program
801 W Fort St, Detroit, MI
313-577-1156
Associate of Applied Science

**Veterinary Technology
Programs, continued**

Minnesota

Argosy University Twin Cities
Veterinary Technician Program
1515 Central Parkway
Eagan, MN   888-844-2004
Associate of Applied Science

Duluth Business University
Veterinary Technology Program
4724 Mike Colalillo Drive
Duluth, MN   800-777-8406
Associate of Applied Science

Globe University
Veterinary Technology Program
8089 Globe Drive
Woodbury, MN 55125
651-714-7360 or 800-231-0660
Associate of Applied Science
Bachelor of Science

Minnesota School of Business-
Blaine
Veterinary Technology Program
3680 Pheasant Ridge Dr NE
Blaine, Minnesota 55449
763-225-8000
Associate of Applied Science

Minnesota School of Business-Elk
River
Veterinary Technology Program
11500 193rd Ave
Elk River, MN   763-367-7000
Associate of Applied Science
Initial Accreditation

Minnesota School of Business-
Lakeville
Veterinary Technology Program
17685 Juniper Path
Lakeville, MN 55044
952-892-9000
Associate in Applied Science
Initial Accreditation

Minnesota School of Business-
Moorhead
2777 34th Street South
Moorhead, MN 56560
218-422-1000
Associate in Applied Science
Initial Accreditation

Minnesota School of Business-
Plymouth
Veterinary Technology Program
1455 County Road 101 North
Plymouth, MN 55447
763-476-2000
Associate of Applied Science
Bachelor of Science

Minnesota School of Business-
Rochester
2521 Pennington Drive NW
Rochester, MN 55901
507-536-9500
Associate of Applied Science

**Veterinary Technology
Programs, continued**

Minnesota School of Business-St
Cloud
Veterinary Technology Program
1201 2nd Street South
Waite Park, MN 56387
320-257-2000
Associate of Applied Science

Ridgewater College
Veterinary Technology Dept.
2101 15th Ave, NW
Willmar, MN 56201
320-222-5200
Associate of Applied Science

Rochester Community and
Technical College
Animal Health Technology
Program
851 30th Avenue SE
Rochester, MN 55904-4999
800-247-1296
Associate of Applied Science

Mississippi

Hinds Community College
Veterinary Technology Program
1100 PMB 11160
Raymond, MS 39154
601-857-3456
Associate of Applied Science

Mississippi State University
240 Wise Drive
Starkville, MS 39762
662-325-3432
Bachelor of Science
Initial Accreditation

Missouri

Brown Mackie College-St Louis
#2 Soccer Park Road
Fenton, MO 63026
636-651-3337
Associate of Applied Science
Initial Accreditation

Crowder College
601 LaClede Avenue
Neosho, MO 64850
417-455-5772
Associate of Applied Science

Jefferson College
1000 Viking Drive
Hillsboro, MO 63050
636-942-3000
Associate of Applied Science

Maple Woods Community College
Veterinary Technology Program
2601 NE Barry Road
Kansas City, MO 64156
816-604-3235
Associate of Applied Science

**Veterinary Technology
Programs, continued**

Midwest Institute
Veterinary Technology Program
962 S Highway Drive
Fenton, MO 63026
800-695-5550
Associate of Occupational Science
Initial Accreditation

The Vet Tech Institute at Hickey
College
Veterinary Technology Program
2780 N Lindbergh
St Louis, MO 63114
314-434-2212
Specialized Associate Degree in
Veterinary Technology

Nebraska

Nebraska College of Technical
Agriculture
Veterinary Technology Program
Curtis, NE 69025
308-367-4124
Associate of Applied Science
Probationary Accreditation

Northeast Community College
Veterinary Technician Program
801 E Benjamin Ave
Norfolk, NE 68702-0469
402-371-2020
Associate of Applied Science

Nevada

The College of Southern Nevada
Veterinary Technology Program
6375 W Charleston Blvd
Las Vegas, NV 89146-1164
702-651-5852
Associate of Applied Science

Pima Medical Institute
Veterinary Technician Program
3333 E Flamingo Road
Las Vegas, NV 89121
702-458-9650
Associate of Applied Science

Truckee Meadows Community
College
Veterinary Technology Program
7000 Dandini Blvd
Reno, NV 89512
775-850-4007
Associate of Applied Science

New Hampshire

Great Bay Community College
Veterinary Technology Program
320 Corporate Drive
Portsmouth, NH 03801
603-427- 7695
Associate in Science

**Veterinary Technology
Programs, continued**

University of New Hampshire
Thompson Sch. of Applied Sc.
Veterinary Technology Program
104A Barton Hall, Durham, NH
603-862-1025
Associate in Applied Science
Initial Accreditation

New Jersey

Bergen Community College
Sch. of Veterinary Technology
400 Paramus Road
Paramus, NJ 07652
201-612-5389
Associate of Applied Science

Camden County College
Animal Science Technology
Program
Blackwood, NJ 08012
856-227-7200
Associate in Animal Technology

New Mexico

Brown Mackie College-
Albuquerque
Veterinary Technology Program
10500 Copper Ave NE
Albuquerque, NM 87123
877-271-3488
Associate of Applied Science
Initial Accreditation

Central New Mexico Community
College
Veterinary Technology Program
525 Buena Vista SE
Albuquerque, NM 87106
505-224-4000
Associate of Applied Science

San Juan College
Veterinary Technology Distance
Learning Program
4601 College Blvd
Farmington, NM 87402
505-566- 3182
Associate of Applied Science

New York

Alfred State College
Veterinary Technology Program
Agriculture Science Building
Alfred, NY 14801
607-578-3009
Associate of Applied Science

Genesee Community College
Veterinary Technology Program
One College Road
Batavia, NY 14020
585-343-0055
Associate of Applied Science
Initial Accreditation

**Veterinary Technology
Programs, continued**

La Guardia Community College
City University of New York
Veterinary Technology Program
31-10 Thomson Ave
Long Island City, NY 11101
718-482-5470
Associate of Applied Science

Medaille College
Veterinary Technology Program
18 Agassiz Cr
Buffalo, NY 14214
716-884-3281
Associate in Science
Bachelor of Science

Medaille College-Rochester
Veterinary Technology Program
1880 South Winton Road
Rochester, NY 14618
585-272-0030
Associate in Applied Science
Initial Accreditation

Mercy College
Veterinary Technology Program
555 Broadway
Dobbs Ferry, NY 10522
914-674-7530
Bachelor of Science

State U. of New York-Canton
Agricultural & Technical Coll.
Veterinary Science Technology
Program
34 Cornell Drive, Canton, NY
315-386-7410
Associate of Applied Science
Bachelor of Science

State U. of New York-Delhi
College of Technology
Veterinary Science Tech. Program
156 Farnsworth Hall
Delhi, NY 13753
607-746-4306
Associate of Applied Science
Bachelor in Business Admin.

State U. of New York-Ulster
Ulster County Comm. College
Veterinary Technology Program
Cottekill Road, Stone Ridge, NY
800-724-0833, ext. 5233
Associate of Applied Science
Probationary Accreditation

Suffolk Community College
Veterinary Science Technology
Program, Western Campus
Crooked Hill Rd, Brentwood NY
631-851- 6289
Associate of Applied Science

**Veterinary Technology
Programs, continued**

Westchester Community College
Veterinary Technology Program
75 Grassland Rd, Valhalla, NY
914-606-6600
Associate of Applied Science
Probationary Accreditation

North Carolina

Asheville-Buncombe Technical
Community College
Veterinary Medical Technology
Program
340 Victoria Rd, Asheville, NC
828-254-1921 ext. 273
Associate of Applied Science

Central Carolina Community
College
Veterinary Medical Technology
Program
1105 Kelly Drive
Sanford, NC 27330
919-775-5401
Associate of Applied Science

Gaston College
Veterinary Medical Technology
Program
201 Hwy 321 South
Dallas, NC 28034-1499
704-922-6200
Associate of Applied Science

Miller-Motte College
Veterinary Technology Program
3901 Capital Blvd, Suite 151
Raleigh, NC 27604
919-855-2504
Diploma Program
Initial Accreditation

North Dakota

North Dakota State University
Veterinary Technology Program
NDSU Dept 2230
PO Box 6050
Fargo, ND 58108
701-231-7511
Bachelor of Science

Ohio

Brown Mackie College-Akron
Veterinary Technology Program
809 White Pond Drive
Akron, OH 44333
330-869-3653
Associate of Applied Science
Initial Accreditation

Brown Mackie College-Cincinnati
1011 Glendale-Milford Road
Cincinnati, OH 45215
513-672-1969
Associate of Science
Probationary Accreditation

**Veterinary Technology
Programs, continued**

Brown Mackie College-Findlay
1700 Fostoria Ave, Suite 100
Findlay, OH 45840
419-423-2211
Associate of Applied Science
Initial Accreditation

Brown Mackie Co.North Canton
Veterinary Technology Program
4300 Munson Street NW
Canton, OH   330-491-8533
Associate of Applied Science
Probationary Accreditation

Columbus State Comm. College
Veterinary Technology Program
550 E Spring St, Columbus, OH
614-287-3685
Associate of Applied Science

Cuyahoga Community College
Veterinary Technology Program
11000 Pleasant Valley Road
Parma, OH 44130
216-987-5450
Associate of Applied Science

Kent State Univ.-Tuscarawas
Sch. of Veterinary Technology
330 University Drive NE
New Philadelphia, OH 44663
330-339-3391
Associate of Applied Science

Miami-Jacobs Career College
Veterinary Technology Program
865 West Market St, Troy, OH
202-336-6780
Associate of Applied Science
Initial Accreditation

UC Blue Ash College
Veterinary Technology Program
Plainfield Rd, Blue Ash, OH
513-936-7173
Associate of Applied Science

Sinclair Community College
Veterinary Technology Program
444 W Third Street, Dayton, OH
937-512-3000
Associate of Applied Science
Initial Accreditation

Stautzenberger College -
Brecksville
Veterinary Technology Program
8001 Katherine Blvd
Brecksville, OH 44141
419-866-0261
Associate of Applied Science

Stautzenberger College-Maumee
Veterinary Technology Program
1796 Indian Wood Circle
Maumee, OH 43537
419-866-0261
Associate of Applied Science

Veterinary Technology Programs, continued

Veterinary Tech Institute at
Bradford School- Columbus
2469 Stelzer Road
Columbus, OH   614-416-6200
Associate of Applied Science

Oklahoma

Heritage College-Oklahoma City
Veterinary Technology Program
7202 S I-35 Service Road
Oklahoma City, OK
405-631-3399
Assoc. of Occupational Studies
Initial Accreditation

Murray State College
Veterinary Technology Program
Tishomingo, OK   580-371-2371
Associate of Applied Science

Oklahoma St.U.- Oklahoma City
Veterinary Technology Program
900 N Portland Ave, Oklahoma
City, OK   405-945-9112
Associate of Applied Science

Tulsa Community College
Veterinary Technology Program
7505 W 41st Street, Tulsa, OK
918-595-8212
Associate of Applied Science

Oregon

Portland Community College
Veterinary Technology Program
Portland, OR   503-244-6111
Associate of Applied Science

Central Oregon Comm. College
Veterinary Technology Program
2600 NW College Way
Bend, OR   541-383-7700
Associate of Applied Science
Initial Accreditation

Pennsylvania

Harcum College
Veterinary Technology Program
750 Montgomery Ave
Bryn Mawr, PA 610-526-6055
Associate in Science

Johnson College
Veterinary Science Technology
Program
3427 N Main Ave, Scranton, PA
800-2WE-WORK,570-342-6404
Associate in Science

Lehigh Carbon & Northampton
Community Colleges
Veterinary Technology Program
Green Pond Rd, Bethlehem, PA
610-861-5548
Associate of Applied Science

**Veterinary Technology
Programs, continued**

Manor College
Veterinary Technology Program
700 Fox Chase Road
Jenkintown, PA 19046
215-885-2360
Associate in Science

The Vet Tech Institute
Veterinary Technician Program
125 Seventh Street
Pittsburgh, PA 15222
412-391-7021 or 800-570-0693
Associate in Specialized
Technology

Wilson College
Veterinary Medical Technology
Program
1015 Philadelphia Ave
Chambersburg, PA 17201
717-264-4141
Bachelor of Science
Probationary Accreditation

YTI Career Institute
Veterinary Technology Program
1405 Williams Road, York, PA
717-295-1100
Associate in Specialized
Technology
Initial Accreditation

Rhode Island

**New England Institute of
Technology**
Veterinary Technology Program
One New England Tech Blvd
East Greenwich, RI 02818
401-467-7744
Associate in Science
Initial Accreditation

South Carolina

Piedmont Technical College
Newberry Campus
1922 Wilson Road
Newberry, SC 29108
803-276-9000
Associate in Health Science

Tri-County Technical College
Veterinary Technology Program
Pendleton, SC 29670
864-646-8361
Associate in Applied Science

Trident Technical College
Veterinary Technology Program
1001 South Live Oak Drive
Moncks Corner, SC 29461
843-899-8011
Associate in Allied Health
Sciences

Veterinary Technology
Programs, continued

South Dakota

Globe University-Sioux Falls
5101 South Broadband Lane
Sioux Falls, SD 57108-2208
715-855-6600 Initial
Accreditation
Associate in Applied Science

National American University
Veterinary Technology Program
Kansas City St, Rapid City, SD
800-843-8892
Associate in Applied Science

Tennessee

Chattanooga State Com. College
4501 Amnicola Highway
Chattanooga, TN   423-697-4400
Associate of Applied Science

Columbia State Com. College
Veterinary Technology Program
Columbia, TN   931-540-2722
Associate of Applied Science

Lincoln Memorial University
Veterinary Medical Technology
Program, Cumberland Gap Pkwy
Harrogate, TN 37752
423-869-6278
Associate/Bachelor of Science

U. of Tennessee at Martin
Veterinary Technology Program
256 Brehm Hall, Martin, TN
731-881-7000
Bachelor of Science
Initial Accreditation

Volunteer State Com. College
Veterinary Technology Program
1480 Nashville Pike
Warf Building Room 100A
Gallatin, TN   615-452-8600
Associate of Applied Science
Initial Accreditation

Texas

Blinn College
301 Post Office St, Bryan, TX
979-209-7597
Associate of Applied Science
Initial Accreditation

Cedar Valley College
Veterinary Technology Program
3030 N Dallas Ave
Lancaster, TX   972-860-8127
Associate of Applied Science
Distance Learning Program

Lone Star College
Veterinary Technology Program
30555 Tomball Pkwy
Tomball, TX   281-351-3357
Associate of Applied Science

Veterinary Technology Programs, continued

McLennan Community College
Veterinary Technology Program
1400 College Drive, Waco, TX
254-299-8750
Associate of Applied Science

Palo Alto College
Veterinary Technology Program
1400 W Villaret Blvd
San Antonio, TX   210-486-3355
Associate of Applied Science

Pima Medical Institute-Houston
Veterinary Technology Program
10201 Katy Freeway
Houston, TX   713-778-0778
Associate of Applied Science
Initial Accreditation

The Vet Tech Institute of Houston
4669 Southwest Freeway
Houston, TX   713-629-1500
Associate of Applied Science

Vista College
Veterinary Technology Program
4620 50th Street, Suite 14
Lubbock, TX   806-785-2100
Associate of Applied Science
Initial Accreditation

Utah

Broadview University – Layton
869 West Hill Field Road
Layton, UT   801-542-8314
Associate of Applied Science

Broadview University- Orem
Veterinary Technology Program
898 North 1200 West
Orem, UT   801-822-5800
Associate of Applied Science
Initial Accreditation

Broadview U. – West Jordan
Veterinary Technician Program
1902 West 7800 South
West Jordan, UT 801-542-7600
Associate of Applied Science

Vermont

Vermont Technical College
Veterinary Technology Program
Randolph Center, VT 05061
802-728-3391
Associate of Applied Science

Virginia

Blue Ridge Community College
Veterinary Technology Program
Weyers Cave, VA 540-234-9261
Associate of Applied Science
Distance Learning

Veterinary Technology
Programs, continued

Northern Virginia Com. College
Veterinary Technology Program
Loudoun Campus
21200 Campus Drive
Sterling, VA   703-450-2525
Associate of Applied Science
Distance Learning Program

Washington

Bellingham Technical College
3028 Lindbergh Ave
Bellingham, WA   360-752-8755
Associate of Applied Science
Initial Accreditation

Pierce College at Fort Steilacoom
Veterinary Technology Program
9401 Farwest Drive, SW
Lakewood, WA   253-964-6668
Assoc. in Veterinary Technology

Pima Medical Institute-Renton
555 S Renton Village Place
Renton, WA   425-228-9600
Associate of Applied Science

Pima Medical Institute-Seattle
Veterinary Technology Program
9709 Third Ave NE, Suite 400
Seattle, WA   800-477- PIMA
Associate of Applied Science

Yakima Valley Com. College
Veterinary Technology Program
Yakima, WA   509-574-4759
Associate of Applied Science

West Virginia

Carver Career Center & Bridge
Valley Com. Technical College
4799 Midland Drive
Charleston, WV   304-348-1965
Associate of Applied Science
Probationary Accreditation

Pierpont Community & Technical
College
Veterinary Technology Program
1201 Locust Ave
Fairmont, WV   304-367-4589
Associate of Applied Science

Wisconsin

Globe University- Appleton
5045 W Grande Market
Grand Chute, WI 54914
920-364-1100
Associate in Applied Science
Initial Accreditation

Globe University-Eau Claire
4955 Bullis Farm Road
Eau Claire, WI   715-855-6600
Associate in Applied Science
Initial Accreditation

**Veterinary Technology
Programs, continued**

Globe University-Green Bay
2620 Development Drive
Green Bay, WI   920-264-1600
Associate in Applied Science
Initial Accreditation

Globe University-La Crosse
Veterinary Technology Program
2651 Midwest Drive
Onalaska, WI   608-779-2600
Associate of Applied Science
Initial Accreditation

Globe University -Madison East
4901 East Park Road
Madison, WI   608-216-9400
Associate in Applied Science
Initial Accreditation

Globe University-Middleton
Veterinary Technology Program
1345 Deming Way
Middleton, WI   608-830-6900
Associate of Applied Science
Initial Accreditation

Globe University-Wausau
Veterinary Technology Program
1480 County Road XX
Rothschild, WI   715-301-1300
Associate in Applied Science
Initial Accreditation

Madison College
Veterinary Technician Program
1701 Wright Street
Madison, WI   608-246-6100
Associate of Applied Science

Milwaukee Career College
Veterinary Technology Program
3077 N Fair Road, Suite 300
Milwaukee, WI   800-754-1009
Associate of Applied Science
Initial Accreditation

Wyoming

Eastern Wyoming College
Veterinary Technology Program
3200 W "C" Street
Torrington, WY 82240
800-658-3195, ext. 8268
Associate in Applied Science

Appendix Three

Animal and Veterinary Organizations

The following list of organizations demonstrates the breadth and depth of the veterinary profession. You may discover by browsing this list that there is a local organization near you which may be of interest to you. You may even be able to acquire some animal and/or veterinary experience at some of these organizations. All of these organizations have websites. To learn more about these organizations, type the name of the organization into a search engine. While this list is not intended to be an all-inclusive list of animal and veterinary organizations, it is long.

Academy of Veterinary Allergy & Clinical Immunology
Academy of Veterinary Emergency & Critical Care Technicians
Academy of Veterinary Homeopathy
Activists of Delaware Valley Animal Network
Adopt a Greyhound
Adopt-A-Greyhound of Central Canada
Akbash Dogs International Rescue Service
Alaska Raptor Rehabilitation Center
Alberta's At-Risk Wildlife
All Creatures Animal Caring Society
Alternative Medicine Our Undeniable Right
Alternatives to Animal Testing Bibliography
American Academy of Veterinary Informatics
American Academy of Veterinary Pharmacology and Therapeutics
American Animal Hlospital Association
American Association for Laboratory Animal Science
American Association of Bovine Practitioners
American Association of Electrodiagnostic Medicine
American Association of Equine Practitioners
American Association of Feline Practitioners
American Association of Pharmaceutical Scientists
American Association of Public Health Veterinarians
American Association of Swine Practitioners
American Association of Veterinary Anatomists
American Association of Veterinary Clinicians
American Association of Veterinary Immunologists
American Association of Veterinary Laboratory Diagnosticians
American Association of Veterinary Medical Colleges
American Association of Veterinary Parasitologists
American Association of Veterinary State Boards

American Association of Wildlife Veterinarians
American Association of Zoo Veterinarians
American Association of Zookeepers
American Biological Safety Association
American Board of Veterinary Toxicology
American Boarding Kennels Association
American Canine Sports Medicine Association
American College of Laboratory Animal Medicine
American College of Theriogenologists
American College of Veterinary Anesthesiologists
American College of Veterinary Clinical Pharmacology
American College of Veterinary Internal Medicine
American College of Veterinary Microbiologists
American College of Veterinary Ophthalmologists
American College of Veterinary Pathologists
American College of Veterinary Preventive Medicine
American College of Veterinary Radiology
American College of Veterinary Surgeons
American Committee on Laboratory Animal Diseases
American Council on Science and Health
American Dairy Goat Association
American Dairy Science Association
American Egg Board
American Fancy Rat and Mouse Association
American Farm Bureau Federation
American Federation of Aviculture
American Feed Industry Association
American Ferret Association
American Fisheries Society
American Humane Association
American Humane Association
American Institute of Fisheries Research Biologists
American Jersey Cattle Association
American Kennel Club
American Meat Institute
American Meat Science Association
American Medical Informatics Association
American Morgan Horse Association
American National Standards Institute
American Ornithologists' Union
American Ostrich Association
American Pet Association, Inc.
American Pet Products Manufacturers Association

American Physiological Society
American Pomeranian Club Breed Rescue
American Pre-Veterinary Medical Association
American Public Health Association
American Quarter Horse Association
American Saddlebred Horse Association
American Sheep Industry Association
American Society for Cell Biology
American Society for Microbiology
American Society for Nutritional Sciences
American Society for Pharmacology and Experimental Therapeutics
American Society for the Prevention of Cruelty to Animals
American Society for Virology
American Society of Agricultural Engineers
American Society of Animal Science
American Society of Ichthyologists and Herpetologists
American Society of Laboratory Animal Practitioners
American Society of Mammalogists
American Society of Parasitologists
American Society of Primatologists
American Society of Tropical Medicine and Hygiene
American Society of Veterinary Ophthalmology
American Tortoise Rescue
American Veterinary Chiropractic Association
American Veterinary Dental College
American Veterinary Distributors Association
American Veterinary Medical Association
American Veterinary Medical Foundation
American Zoo and Aquarium Association
Americans for Medical Progress
Animal Aid
Animal Alliance of Canada
Animal Ark
Animal Behavior and Welfare Sites
Animal Behavior Society
Animal Cruelty Investigation Unit
Animal Emancipation, Inc.
Animal Friends Inc. (Pittsburgh, PA)
Animal Health Distributors Association
Animal Health Information Specialists
Animal Health Institute
Animal Health/Emerging Animal Diseases
Animal Home

Animal and Veterinary Organizations, continued

Animal Industry Foundation
Animal Legal Defense Fund
Animal Liberation Frontline Information Service
Animal Liberation Victoria
Animal People
Animal Productivity & Health Information Network–U.of Prince Edward Is.
Animal Protective League
Animal Protesters' Bulletin
Animal Rescue Kingdom
Animal Rescue League of Boston
Animal Rescue League of Iowa, Inc.
Animal Research Data Base
Animal Responsibility Cyprus
Animal Rights FAQ
Animal Rights Foundation of Florida
Animal Rights Hawaii
Animal Rights Law Center, Rutgers University
Animal Rights News
Animal Rights Resource Site
Animal Trustees of Austin, Inc.
Animal Welfare Institute
Animal-Assisted-Therapy-Team
AnimaLife
Animaline Rescue
Animals Unlimited, Inc.
Anne Arundel County SPCA
Applied Research Ethics National Association
Aquatic Conservation Network
ARK Online
Association for Assessment & Accreditation of Laboratory Animal Care
Association for Biology Laboratory Education
Association for Gnotobiotics
Association for Research in Vision and Ophthalmology
Association for the Study of Animal Behavior
Association for Veterinary Clinical Pharmacology and Therapeutics
Association for Veterinary Informatics
Association of American Feed Control Officials
Association of Avian Veterinarians
Association of Field Ornithologists
Association of Food and Drug Officials
Association of Pet Behavior Counselors
Association of Reptilian & Amphibian Veterinarians
Association of Veterinarians for Animal Rights
Association of Veterinarians for Animal Rights

Animal and Veterinary Organizations, continued

Association of Veterinary Anesthetists
Association of Veterinary Students
Athens Alliance of Allbreed Canine Rescue
Atlantic Salmon Federation
Audubon in New York
Auxiliary to the AVMA
AVMA Network of Animal Health

Bat Conservation International
Bay Area Siberian Husky Rescue Referral
Bear Watch
Beauty without Cruelty India
Because You Care (Erie County, PA)
Berkeley County Humane Society (West Virginia)
Bide-A-Wee Home Association
Biodiversity Conservation Center-West
Biodiversity Forum
Biomedical Research Education Trust
Border Collie Rescue
Boxer Rescue, USA
Brazos Valley Animal Shelter (Texas)
Bristol Exotic and Wild Animal Society

C.L. Davis Foundation for the Advancement of Veterinary and Comparative Pathology
California Biomedical Research Association
California Domestic Ferret Association
Canadian Association for Laboratory Animal Science
Canadian Association of Animal Breeders
Canadian Association of Veterinary Ophthalmology
Canadian Council on Animal Care
Canadian Federation of Humane Societies
Canadian Nature Federation
Canadian Pork Council
Canadian Swine Breeders Association
Canadian Veterinary Medical Association
Canadian World Parrot Trust
Candy Kitchen Rescue Ranch
Canine Companions for Independence
Canine Eye Registration Foundation
Care for the Wild
Carnivore Preservation Trust
Carolina Raptor Center
Cat Fancier's Association

Animal and Veterinary Organizations, continued

Cat Network (St. Louis, MO)
Cats Haven (Indianapolis, IN)
Cats Protection League
Cat's Voice
Celia Hammond Animal Trust
Center for Conservation Biology
Cetacean Society International
Chameleon Conservation Society
Champaign County Humane Society
Chemical Industry Institute of Toxicology
Chicago House Rabbit Society
Christian Veterinary Mission
Christian Veterinary Missions of Canada
College of Veterinarians of Ontario
Colorado Herpetological Society
Colorado Horse Rescue
Colorado Natural Heritage Program
Commonwealth Veterinary Association
Companion Animal Rescue Effort (California)
Companion Greyhounds, Inc.
Compassion in World Farming
Computer-aided Learning in Veterinary Education
Conference of Research Workers in Animal Diseases
Connecticut Cat Rescue Web
Connecticut United for Research Excellence
Conservation Breeding Specialist Group
Conservation Breeding Specialist Group
Consortium of Aquariums Universities & Zoos
Consortium of N. American Veterinary Interactive New Concept Education
Continental Kennel Club
Cornell Research Foundation, Inc.
Council for Agricultural Science and Technology
Council of Docked Breeds
Council on Licensure, Enforcement and Regulation
Cow Liberation Front
Crustacean Society

Dairy Management Inc.
Dallas/Ft. Worth Sheltie Rescue
Darwinian Notions
Days End Farm Horse Rescue
Defenders of Wildlife
Delaware Humane Association
Delaware Veterinary Medical Association

Delta Society
Denver Dumb Friends League (CO)
Dian Fossey Gorilla Fund
Ding Darling Wildlife Society
Doberman Rescue of North Texas
Dogs in Canada Needing Homes
Dolphin Alliance
Donkey Sanctuary
Doris Day Animal League
DragonRidge Net-Refuge of the Rhino
Dreampower Animal Rescue Foundation

EarthCare
Earthkind
Earthtrust Wildlife Conservation Worldwide
East Texas Herpetological Society
Einstein's Online Pet Rescue Group
Elephant Consultancy
Elephant Manager's Association
Elmbrook Humane Society (WI)
Endangered Wildlife Trust
Endocrine Society
English Shepherd Rescue
Entomological Society of America
Ethics and Animals
Ethics Updates Animal Rights
Exotics Sanctuary
Exploits Valley SPCA (Canada)

FARM - Farm Animal Reform Movement
Farm Sanctuary
Federation of American Societies for Experimental Biology
Feline Refuge (Mt. Pleasant, SC)
Feminists for Animal Rights
Feral Cat Coalition
Ferret Home Rescue and Adoption Shelter
Ferret Wise Rescue/Rehabilitation Shelter
Finnish Veterinary Association
Florida Veterinary Medical Association
Food & Drug Law Institute
Foundation for Biomedical Research
Frederick County Humane Society (Maryland)
Frieda's Cat Shelter (Michigan City, IN)
Friends for Life

Friends of Animals Foundation (CA)
Friends of Pets (Ohio)
Friends of the Asian Elephant
Friends of the Environment
Friends of the Sea Otter
Fund for Animals
Fund for the Replacement of Animals in Medical Experiments
Furry Friends Pet Assisted Therapy Services

Georgia Equine Rescue League, Ltd.
German Shorthaired Pointer Rescue
Global Action in Interest of Animals
Goat Veterinary Society
Golden Endings - Golden Retriever Rescue
Golden Gate English Springer Spaniel Rescue
Golden Retriever Rescue of Atlanta
Golden Retriever Rescue, Education and Training (GRREAT)
Gordon Setter Rescue
Gorilla Foundation
Gorilla Haven
Greek Animal Rescue
Green Life Society - North America
Greenpeace International
Greyhound Companions
Greyhound Friends
Greyhound Rescue Group
Greyhounds Anonymous
Guide Dog Foundation for the Blind
Gulf Coast Veterinary Education Foundation

Hawk Cliff Foundation
Hawk Watch International
Hayward Animal Shelter (California)
Heart Bandits - American Eskimo Dog Rescue
Heartland Humane Society (Corvallis, OR)
Herpetologist's League
High North Alliance
Hollydogs Greyhound Adoption
Homeless Cat Network
Hooved Animal Humane Society
Horse Power Projects Inc.
Houston Audubon Society
Houston Homeless Pet Placement League
Human-Animal Bond Association of Canada

Animal and Veterinary Organizations, continued

Humane Innovations and Alternatives
Humane Services of Metro Atlanta
Humane Society of Boulder Valley (Colorado)
Humane Society of Clifton, CO
Humane Society of Fairfax County (Virginia)
Humane Society of Missouri
Humane Society of Ottawa Carleton (Canada)
Humane Society of Ramsey County (Minnesota)
Humane Society of Rochester and Monroe County (New York)
Humane Society of Santa Clara Valley (California)
Humane Society of the Ozarks
Humane Society of the United States
Humane Society of Tucson
Humane Society of Utah
Humanities Organization for Animal and Nature protection
Hunt Saboteurs Association

Idaho Humane Society
In Defense of Animals
Indiana Veterinary Medical Association
Industrial in Vitro Toxicology Group
Infectious Diseases Society of America
Information on Animal Alternatives Database
Institute for International Cooperation in Animal Biologics
Institute for Laboratory Animal Research
Institute of Animal Technology
Institute of International Health
International Academy of Compounding Pharmacists
International Arabian Horse Association
International Association for the Study of Pain
International Association of Agricultural Students
International Association of Equine Practitioners
International Association of Fish and Wildlife Agencies
International Association of Fish and Wildlife Agencies
International Aviculturists Society
International Aviculturists Society
International Center for Aquaculture and Aquatic Environments
International Council for Laboratory Animal Science
International Crane Foundation
International Federation of Placental Associations
International Fund for Animal Welfare
International Generic Horse Association / Horse Aid
International Marine Mammal Association
International Marine life Alliance

Animal and Veterinary Organizations, continued

International Meat and Poultry HACCP Alliance
International Primate Protection League
International Primatological Society
International Rhino Foundation
International Society for Animal Genetics
International Society for Anthrozoology
International Society for Endangered Cats
International Society of Veterinary Perinatology
International Union of Toxicology
International Venomous Snake Society
International Veterinary Acupuncture Society
International Veterinary Biosafety Working Group
International Veterinary Students Association
International Wildlife Coalition
International Wildlife Education & Conservation
Internet Law Library: Legal Treatment of Animals
Internet Zoological Society
Iowa Raptor Foundation
Island Nature Trust
IUCN Cat Specialist Group

Jazz purr Cat Care Society (Canada)
Jews for Animal Rights
Johns Hopkins Center for Alternatives to Animal Testing
Join Hands
Journal of Applied Animal Welfare Science
Journal of the American Veterinary Medical Association
Journal of Veterinary Medical Education

K9 Haven - SF Bay Area Small Breed Rescue
Kansas Animal Welfare Information Collection
Kansas City Pet Adoption League
Kansas Veterinary Medical Association
Kenosha County (WI) Humane Society
Kentucky Humane Society
Kentucky Veterinary Medical Association
Kern Crest Audubon Society
Kitty Love (Scottsdale, AZ)
Kitty Village (Atlanta, GA)
Klee Kai National Kennel Club and Rescue
Kuvasz Rescue
Kyler Laird's Animal Rescue Resources

Animal and Veterinary Organizations, continued

Lab Rescue (Golden Gate Labrador Retriever Club)
Laboratory Animal Science Association
Laboratory Animal Welfare Training Exchange
Labrador Retriever Rescue Contacts
Labrador Retriever Rescue, Inc.
Labrador-L Emergency Medical Assistance
Last Chance for Animals
Latham Foundation
Law Student Animal Rights Alliance
League Against Cruel Sports
League for Animal Welfare
Lepidopterists' Society
Lincolnshire Trust for Nature Conservation
Little Shelter Animal Rescue (NY)
Livestock Behavior, Facility Design and Humane Slaughter
Livestock Conservation Institute
Living Free Animal Sanctuary (Mountain Center, CA)
London Animal Action
Los Angeles SPCA

Mahale Wildlife Conservation Society
Maine Veterinary Medical Association
Make Peace with Animals
Malaria Foundation
Mammal Society
Mammary Gland Physiology and Pathology Society
Manx Nature Conservation Trust
Mare & Foal Sanctuary
Marin Humane Society
Maryland Veterinary Medical Association
Massachusetts Society for Medical Research
Massachusetts Society for the Prevention of Cruelty to Animals Springfield
Animal Shelter
Massachusetts Veterinary Medical Association
Maumee Valley Save-A-Pet (Toledo, OH)
Maxfund Animal Adoption Center (Denver, CO)
Memphis-Shelby County Veterinary Medical Association
Mercy Rescue Net
Merrimack River Feline Rescue Society
Michigan Animal Rescue League
Michigan Greyhound Connection
Mid-Continent Association for Agriculture, Biomedical Research and
Education
Milford, MA Humane Society

Animal and Veterinary Organizations, continued

Minnesota Veterinary Medical Association
MISMR - Michigan Society for Medical Research
Missing and Found Animal Pages (USDA - APHIS)
Mississippi Animal Rescue League
Monmouth County SPCA (New Jersey)
Montgomery County Society for the Prevention of Cruelty to Animals
Morris Animal Foundation

Nashville Humane Association
National 4-H Council
National Alternative Livestock Association
National Animal Interest Alliance
National Animal Poison Control Center
National Anti-Hunt Campaign
National Anti-Vivisection Society
National Association for Biomedical Research
National Association of Animal Breeders
National Association of Professional Pet Sitters
National Association of State Departments of Agriculture
National Audubon Society
National Bison Association
National Cattlemen's Beef Association
National Contract Poultry Growers Association
National Dairy Herd Improvement Association
National Farmers Organization
National Farmers Union
National Fisheries Institute
National Foundation for Infectious Diseases
National Institute for Control of Veterinary Bioproducts & Pharmaceuticals
National Livestock Producers Association
National Mastitis Council
National Meat Association
National Milk Producers Federation
National Parks and Conservation Association
National Pedigreed Livestock Council
National Pork Producers Council
National Society for Histotechnology
National Turkey Federation
National Turtle and Tortoise Society
National Wildlife Federation
Native Fish Society

Natural Resources Defense Council
Nature Conservancy
Nature Conservancy of Hawaii
Naturenet
Nebraska Humane Society
Neponset Valley Humane Society (Massachusetts)
New Hampshire Doberman Rescue League
New Hampshire Equine Humane Association
New Hampshire Society for the Prevention of Cruelty to Animals
New Mexico Veterinary Medical Association
New Mexico Wildlife Association
New York State House Rabbit Society
Noah's Arc (TN)
Noah's Ark Animal Foundation
Noah's Ark Rehabilitation Center (Locust Grove, GA)
NORINA Database (Audiovisual Alternatives to Laboratory Animals in Teaching)
North American Border Collie Rescue Network
North American Equine Ranching Information Council
North American Native Fishes Association
North American Vegetarian Society
North American Veterinary College Administrators
North American Veterinary Technician Association
North Carolina Veterinary Medical Association
North Shore Animal League (New York)
North Texas Weimaraner Club - Rescue
North Valley Veterinary Technician Association
Northampton County, PA SPCA
Norwegian Reference Centre for Laboratory Animal Science & Alternatives
Nova Scotia Bird Society

Ocean Voice International
Ontario Association of Veterinary Technicians
Ontario Veterinary Medical Association
Open Your Heart (NJ)
Operation Kindness No Kill Animal Shelter (Carrollton, TX)
Oregon Biomedical Research Association
Oregon Humane Society
Organization of Biological Field Stations
Orlando Humane Society/SPCA of Central Florida
Ornithology and Nature Conservation in the Balearic Islands
Orphaned Wildlife Rehabilitation Society
Orthopedic Foundation for Animals
Orthopedists' Society

Pacific Rivers Council
PawSafe Animal Rescue
Peninsula Humane Society (San Mateo, CA)
Pennsylvania Ferret Rescue Association
Pennsylvania Society for Biomedical Research
People Against Chimpanzee Experiments
Performing Animal Welfare Society
Pet Action League (Central Florida)
Pet Adoption (Mining Company)
Pet Adoption Fund (Canoga Park, CA)
Pet Connection (Blount County Eastern Tennessee)
Pet Industry Joint Advisory Council
PETA Online
PetLine Lost & Found Service
PetNet, A Network of Animal Shelters
Pets Are Wonderful Support
Pets in Need (Redwood City, CA)
Pets Scoop
PetWhere Animal Tracking Software
Pharmachem Online
PhillyPAWS
Pigs Sanctuary
Pinellas Animal Foundation
Pisces
Placer County SPCA (CA)
Poultry Science Association
Pound Rescue of Athens Ohio
Predator Defense Institute
Primarily Primates
Primate Information Center
Primate Supply Information Clearinghouse
Progressive Animal Welfare Society (Washington)
Project BREED (Breed Rescue Efforts and Education)
Project Equus
Protectors of Animals, Inc. (CT)
Protesters Animal Information Network
Psychologists for the Ethical Treatment of Animals
Public Responsibility in Medicine and Research
Purrfect Pals Cat Shelter

R.E.S.C.U.E (Maricopa County - AZ)
Radiological Society of North America
Ragdoll Cat Rescue
Ranger's Realtime Rescue

Animal and Veterinary Organizations, continued

Raptor Repertoire
Raptor Research Foundation, Inc.
Rat and Mouse Club of America
Registry of Comparative Pathology
Registry of Comparative Pathology
Rescue A Shar-Pei (Illinois/Indiana)
Research Defense Society
Respect for Animals
Rhode Island Veterinary Medical Association
Richmond SPCA (Virginia)
Rocky Mountain Animal Defense
Rottweiler Rescue of Mid-Michigan
Rottweilers Needing Homes

Safari Club International
San Diego Animal Advocates
San Diego County Animal Shelters
San Francisco SPCA
San Luis Obispo Animal Requesting Friends (California)
Sanctuary for Animals (Westtown, NY)
Santa Barbara Wildlife Care Network
Save a Sato
Save Our Critters Society (Washington)
Save our Squirrel Glider Possum
Save The Horse, Inc.
Save the Manatee Club
Save the Rhino International
Saving Berries for the Bears
Scientists' Center for Animal Welfare
Second Chance Pet Adoptions (North Carolina)
Shea Park - Safe Haven for Endangered Animals Exotic Animal Sanctuary
Sierra Club
Silver Lake Animal Rescue League (MI)
Society and Animals
Society for Conservation Biology (University of Texas Austin)
Society for Cryobiology
Society for In Vitro Biology
Society for Integrative and Comparative Biology
Society for the Study of Amphibians and Reptiles
Society for the Study of Amphibians and Reptiles
Society for the Study of Reproduction
Society for Theriogenology
Society for Tropical Veterinary Medicine
Society for Veterinary Medical Ethics

Society of Environmental Toxicology and Chemistry
Society of Marine Mammalogists
Society of Practicing Veterinary Surgeons
Society of Protozoologists
Society of Toxicologic Pathologists
Society of Toxicology
Somali & Abyssinian Breed Rescue & Education
SOS Rhino
Support for Research on Alternatives to Animal Use in Research & Testing
South Plains Wildlife Rehabilitation Center, Inc.
Southampton Animal Control (New York)
Southwest Foundation for Biomedical Research
SPCA of Anne Arundel County (Maryland)
SPCA of Texas
St. Francis Wildlife
St. Johns County Audubon Society
Standard Schnauzer Club Rescue
Stanley Park Ecology Society (Vancouver, BC)
Strays Halfway House
Street Cats Rescue Society of Alberta (Canada)
Student Veterinary Emergency and Critical Care Society
Student Veterinary Zoological Information Exchange
Students for Animal Liberation
Suffolk County, New York SPCA
Suncoast Bulldog Friends
Suncoast Seabird Sanctuary

Tarrant County Purebred Cat Rescue - Dallas/Ft. Worth Texas
Teaming With Wildlife
Tennessee Equine Veterinary Research Organization
Teratology Society
Texas Dairy Herd Improvement Association
Texas Pet Bird Rescue
Texas Veterinary Medical Association
Three "R's" of Animal Testing Alternatives
Toronto Vegetarian Association
TreeHouse Animal Foundation
Tri-County Collie Rescue (MI)
Tria-Valley Animal Rescue (California)
Trojan Horse of Animal Protectionism
Trout Unlimited Canada
Turpentine Creek Exotic Wildlife Refuge

Animal and Veterinary Organizations, continued

U.S. Pharmacopeia
Union of Concerned Scientists
United Egg Producers
United Poultry Concerns
United States Animal Health Association
United States Dressage Federation
Universities Federation for Animal Welfare
Upper Valley Humane Society (NH)
USA DOG (Defenders of Greyhounds)
USDA-NAL Animal Welfare Information Center

Vegan Action
Vegetarian Resource Center
Vegetarian Resource Group
VETAIR Foundation
Veterinary Association for Arbitration and Jurisprudence
Veterinary Cancer Society
Veterinary Educational Team Sled Dog Racing
Veterinary Emergency Critical Care Society
Veterinary History Society
Veterinary Information Network
Veterinary Medical Association of New York City, Inc.
Veterinary Medical Libraries Section - Medical Library Association
Veterinary Technician Anesthetist Society
Virginia Veterinary Medical Association
Viva Vegetarians International Voice for Animals
Volunteers for Animal Welfare, Inc. (Oklahoma City, OK)

Washington D.C. Humane Society
Washington Ornithological Society
Washington Protection Association
Washington State Veterinary Medical Association
West Point Veterinary Medical Society
West Suburban Humane Society (Chicago, IL)
West Virginia Raptor Rehabilitation Center
Western Canadian Veterinary Students' Association
Whidbey Animals' Improvement Foundation (Washington)
Whiskers Animal Benevolent League (NY)
Wild About Cats
Wilding Heritage Farm
Wildlife Conservation Society (Bronx Zoo)
Wildlife Disease Association
Wildlife Preservation Trust International
Wildlife Waystation

Animal and Veterinary Organizations, continued

Winn Feline Foundation
Winnipeg Humane Society
Wisconsin Chow Chow Rescue
Wisconsin Humane Society
World Animal Net Directory
World Aquaculture Society
World Association for Buiatrics
World Association of Veterinary Educators
World Federation of Parasitologists
World Small Animal Veterinary Association
World Society for the Protection of Animals Animals
World Veterinary Association
World Wildlife Fund
World Wildlife Fund - Canada
WWW Virtual Library: Animal health, well-being, and rights
WWW Virtual Library: Biology Societies and Organizations

Appendix Four

VMCAS Application Questions

The following questions are some of the questions asked on the VMCAS Application. This condensed list represents the more essential questions (multiple address and phone number questions, for example, are not included below). The questions are truncated for space and ease of reading and appear on the VMCAS form in a different order than below.

Personal Information
Name, addresses, phone numbers, email, etc.
State/Provincial Residency, Citizenship, DOB, etc.

Your Background Information
Current student status? Self-reported GPA?
Has there been any interval longer than 3 months during which you were not employed or enrolled as a student? If yes, explain.
Have you ever received any action for poor academic performance or conduct violation? If yes, fully explain.
Have you ever received a felony or misdemeanor conviction other than a minor traffic violation? If yes, fully explain.
Parental information names and addresses. State residency.

Your Enrollment Information
This is a table of questions about all college level enrollment including: name of institution(s), dates of enrollment, degree earned or expected, date(s) of degree earned, major, and 'is this your primary institution?'
Note: No college enrollments may be left out – without serious consequence. It may be to your disadvantage if you enroll at numerous institutions, especially if your enrollments are on a part-time status.

Your Academic Coursework
There is an extensive table of questions about all coursework ever taken at the college level. No coursework may be left off this table – without serious consequence. Questions include: name of institution, dates of attendance, credit/units/hours, grade/mark, course title, prerequisite course designation.

VMCAS Application Questions, continued

Your Animal/Veterinary Experiences

Dates of experience?
Description of duties?
Average number of hours per week?
Total number of hours over span of experience?
Animal Types: small animal, food animal, equine, mixed animal, research, zoo/wildlife, exotic/avian?
Name of Evaluator/Supervisor?
(You must complete this set of questions for each experience.)

Your Employment Experiences

Do not include experience listed in Animal Experience
Dates of experience?
Description of duties?
Average number of hours per week?
Total number of hours over span of experience?
(You must complete this set of questions for each experience.)

Your Extracurricular Activities, Honors or Awards

Briefly describe any honors or awards you received.
Briefly describe any Extracurricular or Community Activities you had, including dates of activities.

Your Previous Applications

List all graduate and professional programs to which you were accepted. Indicate: enrollment, deferred enrollment, declined offer, withdrew, suspended, dismissed. There is another similar question about applying to veterinary medicine programs.
Note: VMCAS participating veterinary schools to which you apply can see all of the other veterinary schools to which you applied. While this may appear inappropriate to share with all veterinary schools to which an applicant applies, it is legal to ask and to share this information among the veterinary schools.

Your Personal Statement

The following are the words as stated on the VMCAS application. "The personal statement should help the admission committee(s) learn something personal about the applicant, about his or her interest in veterinary medicine, and about your career goals."

Appendix Five

Letter of Evaluation Questions

While the following information is not copyright protected, please know the following summary is the work of the AAVMC. This author and many are grateful to the AAVMC for not restricting use of this information.

Only the most important VMCAS evaluation questions are presented in our summary. (Contact information, for example, are omitted. Those schools which do not participate in VMCAS will have their own forms with other questions.

The following questions have been asked of the evaluator/recommender:

In what capacity have you known the candidate?

How long have you known the candidate?
Author's Comment: Longer periods of time improve the strength of the letter. 200-300 hours (minimum) are recommended for a strong letter.

Statement: '…please indicate your assessment of the candidate in each category [below].' *Each of the following questions has a fifth option of 'Have not observed,' which we chose not to list.*

Initiative/Originality
1. Needs occasional prodding
2. Does assigned work of own accord
3. Completes suggested extra work
4. Original, independent, imaginative

Motivation (for becoming a Veterinarian)
1. Is uncertain of career goals
2. Simply wants to be a professional (any type)
3. Dedicator worker
4. Is among the most motivated

Intellectual capacity
1. Below average
2. Average
3. Above average
4. Exceptional intellectual capacity

Letter of Evaluation Questions, continued

Personal and social maturity
1. Below average
2. Average maturity
3. Above average
4. Exceptionally mature

Dependability and reliability
1. Doubtful reliability
2. Usually reliable
3. Above average reliability
4. Unquestionable reliability

Emotional stability
1. Very excitable
2. Easily upset
3. Usually stable, poised
4. Stable, well balanced

Leadership
1. Satisfied to follow
2. Occasionally a leader
3. Frequently a leader
4. Outstanding leader

Ability to work with others
1. Lacks interpersonal skills
2. Occasionally uncooperative
3. Works well with others
4. Excellent interpersonal skills

Character and integrity
1. Untrustworthy
2. Occasionally compromises ethics for personal gain
3. No serious flaws in ethics or integrity
4. Absolutely trustworthy, observes high-quality ethics

Verbal Skills
1. Below average
2. Moderately articulate
3. Above average
4. Articulate, clear, fluent

Letter of Evaluation Questions, continued

Acceptance of feedback and instruction
1. Resistant to constructive feedback
2. Sometimes resistant to feedback
3. Accepts feedback
4. Seeks out feedback

Ability to handle animals
1. Below average
2. Acceptable ability with small animals
3. Acceptable ability with large animals
4. Acceptable ability with small and large animals

Please rate this applicant's overall potential

1. Below average, bottom 40%
2. Average Middle 20%
3. Above Average, Next 15%
4. Good, Next Highest 15%
5. Very good, Next Highest 4%
6. Outstanding, Next Highest 4%
7. Truly Exceptional, Next Highest 2%

Kindly attach a letter of recommendation.

Appendix Six

Colleges with Agricultural Programs

PreVetAdvising.com has compiled a list of undergraduate colleges and universities with agricultural programs. Virtually all of these institutions will have Animal Science Programs. If you do not have large animal experience and it is unlikely you could gain large animal experience near your home, you may want to attend a college where you could gain animal husbandry skills with large animals. We recommend you attend the most competitive college to which you could gain admission.

Colleges and universities with agricultural and animal science programs tend to have better pre-veterinary advising than most other institutions. This is especially true when comparing the following colleges to small liberal arts colleges where there may not be a full-time pre-health advisor.

Canada
McGill University   Montreal, Canada
University of Guelph   Guelph, Canada

Puerto Rico
University of Puerto Rico   San Juan, PR

Alabama
Alabama A & M University   Normal, AL
Auburn University   Auburn University, AL
Tuskegee University   Tuskegee Institute, AL

Arkansas
Arkansas State University   State University, AR
University of Arkansas Main Campus   Fayetteville, AR

Arizona
University of Arizona   Tucson, AZ

California
Cal Poly State U-San Luis Obispo   San Luis Obispo, CA
Cal State Polytechnic U-Pomona   Pomona, CA
Shasta College   Redding, CA
University of California-Davis   Davis, CA

Colleges with Agricultural Programs, continued

Colorado
Bel-Rea Institute of Animal Tech.   Denver, CO
Colorado State University   Fort Collins, CO
T H Pickens Technical Center   Aurora, CO
University of Denver   Denver, CO

Connecticut
University of Connecticut   Storrs, CT

Delaware
Delaware State University   Dover, DE
University of Delaware   Newark, DE

Florida
University of Florida   Gainesville, FL

Georgia
Berry College   Mount Berry, GA
Fort Valley State University   Fort Valley, GA
University of Georgia   Athens, GA

Hawaii
University of Hawaii at Manoa   Honolulu, HI

Iowa
Dordt College   Sioux Center, IA
Iowa State University   Ames, IA
Iowa Western CCl-Clarinda   Clarinda, IA

Idaho
Brigham Young University-Idaho   Rexburg, ID
University of Idaho   Moscow, ID

Illinois
Black Hawk College-East Campus   Kewanee, IL
Shawnee College   Ullin, IL
Southern Illinois U-Carbondale   Carbondale, IL
U Illinois-Urbana Champaign   Champaign, IL

Indiana
Purdue University   West Lafayette, IN

Kansas
Kansas State University   Manhattan, KS

Colleges with Agricultural Programs, continued

Kentucky
University of Kentucky   Lexington, KY

Louisiana
Louisiana Technical University   Ruston, LA
LSU A&M-Baton Rouge   Baton Rouge, LA

Massachusetts
Hampshire College   Amherst, MA
Mount Ida College   Newton Centre, MA
University of Massachusetts Amherst Amherst, MA

Maryland
University of Maryland College Park College Park, MD

Maine
University of Maine at Orono   Orono, ME

Michigan
Andrews University   Berrien Springs, MI
Michigan State University   East Lansing, MI

Minnesota
Minnesota WCTC-Worthington   Worthington, MN
Minnesota WCTC-Jackson   Jackson, MN
Mesabi Range CTC -Virginia   Virginia, MN
South Central Technical College-Mankato North Mankato, MN
University of Minnesota-Twin Cities Minneapolis, MN

Missouri
Clinton Technical School   Clinton, MO
College of the Ozarks   Point Lookout, MO
Missouri State University   Springfield, MO
Northwest Missouri State University Maryville, MO
Rolla Technical Institute   Rolla, MO
Truman State University   Kirksville, MO
University of Missouri-Columbia   Columbia, MO
Wentworth Military Academy   Lexington, MO

Mississippi
Mississippi State University   Mississippi State, MS

Montana
Montana State University-Bozeman   Bozeman, MT

North Carolina
NC Agricultural & Technical State U.   Greensboro, NC
NC State University at Raleigh   Raleigh, NC

North Dakota
North Dakota State University   Fargo, ND

Nebraska
University of Nebraska-Lincoln   Lincoln, NE
Vatterott College   Omaha, NE

New Hampshire
University of New Hampshire   Durham, NH

New Jersey
Rutgers-State University of NJ   New Brunswick, NJ

New Mexico
New Mexico State University   Las Cruces, NM

Nevada
University of Nevada-Reno   Reno, NV

New York
Cornell University   Ithaca, NY
CUNY Hunter College   New York, NY
SUNY Morrisville   Morrisville, NY
SUNY Cobleskill   Cobleskill, NY

Ohio
Ohio State University-Columbus   Columbus, OH

Oklahoma
Cameron University   Lawton, OK
Oklahoma Panhandle State University   Goodwell, OK
Oklahoma State University   Stillwater, OK
Langston University   Langston, OK

Oregon
Oregon State University   Corvallis, OR

Colleges with Agricultural Programs, continued

Pennsylvania
Delaware Valley College   Doylestown, PA
Penn State-University Park   University Park, PA

Rhode Island
University of Rhode Island   Kingston, RI

South Carolina
Clemson University   Clemson, SC

South Dakota
Si Tanka University at Huron   Huron, SD
South Dakota State University   Brookings, SD

Tennessee
Middle Tennessee State University   Murfreesboro, TN
University of Tennessee-Knoxville   Knoxville, TN

Texas
Abilene Christian University   Abilene, TX
Angelo State University   San Angelo, TX
Hardin-Simmons University   Abilene, TX
Prairie View A&M University   Prairie View, TX
Sam Houston State University   Huntsville, TX
Southwestern University   Georgetown, TX
Stephen F Austin State University   Nacogdoches, TX
Sul Ross State University   Alpine, TX
Tarleton State University   Stephenville, TX
Texas A&M University-Commerce   Commerce, TX
Texas A&M University-Kingsville   Kingsville, TX
Texas A&M University-Main Camps   College Station, TX
Texas State University-San Marcos   San Marcos, TX
Texas Tech. University   Lubbock, TX
West Texas A&M University   Canyon, TX

Utah
Utah State University   Logan, UT

Virginia
Virginia Polytechnic Inst.   Blacksburg, VA

Vermont
University of Vermont   Burlington, VT

Colleges with Agricultural Programs, continued

Washington

Washington State University	Pullman, WA
Yakima Valley Comm. College	Yakima, WA

Wisconsin

Lakeshore Technical College	Cleveland, WI
University of Wisconsin-Baraboo-Sauk	Baraboo, WI
University of Wisconsin-Barron County	Rice Lake, WI
University of Wisconsin-Fox Valley	Menasha, WI
University of Wisconsin-Madison	Madison, WI
University of Wisconsin-Manitowoc	Manitowoc, WI
University of Wisconsin-Marathon City	Wausau, WI
University of Wisconsin-Platteville	Platteville, WI
University of Wisconsin-River Falls	River Falls, WI
University of Wisconsin-Rock County	Janesville, WI
University of Wisconsin-Waukesha	Waukesha, WI

West Virginia

West Virginia University	Morgantown, WV

Wyoming

University of Wyoming	Laramie, WY

While we believe our list above is complete, there may be a new college of agriculture which we have not included. If you know of one not on our list above, please let us know by email at: assistant@PreVetAdvising.com.

Appendix Seven

Recommended Pre-Veterinary Colleges

PreVetAdvising.com maintains a list of undergraduate colleges and universities that offer good pre-veterinary preparation. There are six criteria that an institution must meet to be listed. Briefly stated, to be listed, a pre-veterinary program must:

- Have an advisor who is a member of the National Association of Advisors for the Health Professions (NAAHP.org) or one of its regional associations;
- Have a vibrant pre-veterinary or pre-health club that is officially recognized by a student activities office or similar campus entity;
- Offer all of the basic science courses discussed in Chapter One on an annual basis;
- Offer Genetics, Microbiology, and Statistics as well as the courses listed on page 14 every other year if not annually;
- Be a selective four-year college and offer a four-year degree program in which all of the above-mentioned courses may apply toward that four-year degree; and
- (Should) Maintain a list of veterinarians (and organizations) with whom pre-veterinary students may gain animal or veterinary experience.

A college or university cannot purchase a spot on our list. They either meet the criteria or they do not. Evaluation for inclusion is done solely by PreVetAdvising.com and we have sole discretion in determining which colleges are placed on our list. Canadian and international undergraduate institutions are welcome to apply for inclusion in our list of recommended colleges. The free application is at: PreVetAdvising.com/index.php/forms.

Please check our website as some schools may be taken off the list and others may be added. If you visit a college and find evidence, for example, that a pre-veterinary or pre-health club no longer exists, please contact us at: assistant@PreVetAdvising.com.

If you are an advisor or college administrator and wish to be added to our recommended list of colleges, a free application may be obtained at: assistant@PreVetAdvising.com. Please send us all of your contact information in your email request.

Recommended Pre-Veterinary Colleges

Alabama
Auburn University, Auburn
Auburn University, Montgomery
Birmingham-Southern College
Tuskegee University
University of Alabama
University of Alabama at Birmingham
University of Mobile
University of North Alabama
University of South Alabama

Alaska
University of Alaska, Fairbanks

Arkansas
University of Arkansas

Arizona
Arizona State University, Phoenix
Arizona State University, Tempe
Northern Arizona University
University of Arizona, Tucson

California
California Institute of Technology
California Polytechnic State University
California State University, Dominguez Hills
California State University, Fresno
California State University, Fullerton
California State University, Long Beach
California State University, Northridge
California State University, Sacramento
Pomona College
San Diego State University
San Francisco State University
Stanford University
University of California, Berkeley
University of California, Davis
University of California, Irvine

Recommended Pre-Veterinary Colleges, continued

University of California, Los Angeles
University of California, Merced
University of California, Riverside
University of California, San Diego
University of California, Santa Barbara
University of California, Santa Cruz
University of San Diego
University of San Francisco
University of Southern California
Western University of Health Sciences

Colorado
Colorado State University, Fort Collins
Colorado State University, Pueblo
United States Air Force Academy
University of Colorado at Boulder
University of Colorado, Denver
University of Denver

Connecticut
Central Connecticut State University
Connecticut College
Southern Connecticut State University
University of Connecticut, Storrs
University of Hartford
Western Connecticut State University
Yale University

Delaware
University of Delaware

District of Columbia
George Washington University
Georgetown University
University of the District of Columbia

Florida
Florida Atlantic University
Florida Institute of Technology
Florida International University
Florida State University
Miami University
Palm Beach Atlantic University
University of Central Florida

Recommended Pre-Veterinary Colleges, continued

University of Florida, Gainesville
University of Miami
University of South Florida
University of Tampa
University of West Florida

Georgia
Georgia Institute of Technology
Spellman College
University of Georgia

Hawaii
Hawaii Pacific University
University of Hawaii, Manoa
University of Honolulu

Idaho
Idaho State University
The College of Idaho
University of Idaho

Illinois
DePaul University
Eastern Illinois University
Illinois College
Illinois Institute of Technology
Illinois State University
Illinois Wesleyan University
Loyola University Chicago
Southern Illinois University
University of Illinois at Chicago
University of Illinois at Urbana-Champaign
Western Illinois University

Indiana
Indiana University Northwest
Indiana University, Bloomington
Marian College, Indianapolis
Purdue University
University of Indianapolis
University of Notre Dame
University of Southern Indiana

Recommended Pre-Veterinary Colleges, continued

Iowa
Iowa State University
University of Iowa
University of Northern Iowa

Kansas
Kansas State University
University of Kansas
Wichita State University

Kentucky
Eastern Kentucky University
University of Kentucky

Louisiana
Centenary College of Louisiana
Louisiana State University
Tulane University
Xavier University of Louisiana

Maine
University of Maine, Farmington
University of Maine, Orono

Maryland
Johns Hopkins University
University of Maryland, Baltimore County
University of Maryland, College Park
University of Maryland -Baltimore

Massachusetts
Amherst College
Boston College
Boston University
Dartmouth College
Harvard University
Massachusetts College of Pharmacy & Health Sciences
Smith College
Tufts University
University of Massachusetts, Amherst
University of Massachusetts, Boston
University of Massachusetts, Dartmouth
University of Massachusetts, Lowell

Recommended Pre-Veterinary Colleges, continued

Michigan
Central Michigan University
Kalamazoo College
Michigan State University
Michigan Technological University
Northern Michigan University
University of Michigan Ann Arbor
University of Michigan Dearborn
Western Michigan University

Minnesota
Minnesota State University Moorhead
University of Minnesota

Mississippi
Jacksonville State University
Mississippi State University
Mississippi Valley State University

Missouri
Missouri Baptist University
Missouri University of Science and Technology
Missouri Western State University
University of Missouri, Columbia
University of Missouri, Kansas City
Washington University, Saint Louis

Montana
University of Montana, Missoula

Nebraska
Nebraska Wesleyan University
University of Nebraska, Kearney
University of Nebraska, Lincoln

Nevada
University of Nevada, Las Vegas
University of Nevada, Reno

New Hampshire
University of New Hampshire

Recommended Pre-Veterinary Colleges, continued

New Jersey
New Jersey Institute of Technology
Princeton University
Ramapo College of New Jersey
Richard Stockton College of New Jersey
Rutgers University
Seton Hall University

New Mexico
St. John's College, Santa Fe
University of New Mexico

New York
Canisius College
Clarkson University
Colgate University
Columbia University
Cornell University
CUNY Queens College
CUNY Hunter College
Fordham University
Hofstra University
Le Moyne College
Long Island University
Nazareth College
New York University
Niagara University
Rensselaer Polytechnic Institute
St. Bonaventure University
St. John's University
St. Lawrence University
SUNY Geneseo
SUNY University at Albany
SUNY University at Binghamton
SUNY University at Buffalo
SUNY University at Stony Brook
Suffolk University
Syracuse University
Vassar College
Yeshiva University

Recommended Pre-Veterinary Colleges, continued

North Carolina
Davidson College
Duke University
North Carolina State University
University of North Carolina, Asheville
University of North Carolina, Chapel Hill
University of North Carolina, Charlotte
University of North Carolina, Greensboro
University of North Carolina, Pembroke
University of North Carolina, Wilmington

North Dakota
North Dakota State University

Ohio
Case Western Reserve University
Kent State University
Ohio State University
Ohio Wesleyan University
University of Cincinnati
University of Dayton
University of Toledo

Oklahoma
Southwestern Oklahoma State University
University of Central Oklahoma
University of Oklahoma
University of Tulsa

Oregon
Eastern Oregon University
Oregon State University
Portland State University
Southern Oregon University
University of Portland

Recommended Pre-Veterinary Colleges, continued

Pennsylvania
Bryn Mar College
Carnegie Mellon University
Drexel University, Philadelphia
Franklin and Marshall College
Indiana University of Pennsylvania
Lehigh University
Muhlenberg College
Pennsylvania State University, Brandywine
Pennsylvania State, Altoona
Pennsylvania State Erie/Behrend College
Pennsylvania State University, State College
Pittsburg State University
Shippensburg University
Susquehanna University
Temple University
University of Pennsylvania
University of Pittsburgh
University of Pittsburgh, Johnstown
University of Scranton
University of the Sciences, Philadelphia
Villanova University
West Chester University of Pennsylvania

Rhode Island
Brown University
University of Rhode Island

South Carolina
Clemson University

South Dakota
South Dakota State University
University of South Dakota

Tennessee
East Tennessee State University
Middle Tennessee State University
Tennessee Tech University
The University of Memphis
University of Tennessee, Chattanooga
University of Tennessee, Knoxville

Recommended Pre-Veterinary Colleges, continued

Texas
Mt San Antonio College
Rice University
Sam Houston State University
Texas A&M University, College Station
Texas A&M University, Kingsville
Texas State University, San Marcos
University of Dallas
University of Houston
University of North Texas
University of Texas at Arlington
University of Texas at Austin
University of Texas at Brownsville
University of Texas at Dallas
University of Texas at El Paso
University of Texas at San Antonio

Utah
Brigham Young University, Provo
Brigham Young University, Rexburg
Southern Utah University
University of Utah
Utah State University, Logan
Utah Valley University, Orem

Vermont
Middlebury College
University of Vermont

Virginia
College of William and Mary
George Mason University, Fairfax
George Mason University, Manassas
University of Richmond
University of Virginia
Virginia Commonwealth University
Virginia Military Institute
Virginia Polytechnic Institute and State University

Recommended Pre-Veterinary Colleges, continued

Washington
Seattle Pacific University
Seattle University
University of Washington
Washington State University
Washington State University, Vancouver
Western Washington University

West Virginia
West Virginia University

Wisconsin
University of Wisconsin, Eau Claire
University of Wisconsin, Kenosha
University of Wisconsin, Madison
University of Wisconsin, Madison
University of Wisconsin, Milwaukee
University of Wisconsin, Parkside

Wyoming
University of Wyoming

76379241R00121

Made in the USA
Lexington, KY
20 December 2017